BLACK AND WHITE

BLACK AND WHITE

The Way I See It

RICHARD WILLIAMS

WITH BART DAVIS

ATRIA BOOKS

New York London Toronto Sydney New Delhi

 **ATRIA** BOOKS
A Division of Simon & Schuster, Inc.
1230 Avenue of the Americas
New York, NY 10020

First Atria Books hardcover edition May 2014

ATRIA BOOKS and colophon are trademarks of Simon & Schuster, Inc.

For information about special discounts for bulk purchases,
please contact Simon & Schuster Special Sales at 1-866-506-1949
or business@simonandschuster.com.

The Simon & Schuster Speakers Bureau can bring authors to your
live event. For more information or to book an event contact the
Simon & Schuster Speakers Bureau at 1-866-248-3049
or visit our website at www.simonspeakers.com.

Interior design by Jill Putorti
Jacket design by Min Choi
Jacket photographs by Getty Images except middle photo on left by
Alese O. Pechter

Manufactured in the United States of America

10 9 8 7 6 5 4 3 2 1

Library of Congress Cataloging-in-Publication Data is available.

ISBN 978-1-4767-0420-3
ISBN 978-1-4767-0422-7 (ebook)

For Julia Metcalf Williams,
my greatest hero

I am the darker brother.
They send me to eat in the kitchen
When company comes,
But I laugh,
And eat well,
And grow strong.

LANGSTON HUGHES

CONTENTS

X CONTENTS

BLACK AND WHITE

CHAPTER ONE

Wimbledon is a special place for me. It's the tennis tournament where my daughters, Venus and Serena, have won the Ladies' Singles Championship ten years out of the past twelve. Yet, on that rainy Saturday morning in August 2012, anxiously looking down from our family box while Serena played her finals match on center court, I couldn't help thinking that we almost didn't make it here at all.

Wimbledon is the oldest tennis tournament in the world, first played in 1877. It is the grandest of the four Grand Slams—including the French Open, the Australian Open, and the U.S. Open. It's the only one still played on grass, the game's first surface, the reason it was originally called "lawn tennis." Yet, with the terrible illnesses and foot problems Serena suffered in the past year, I never dreamed I'd be watching her compete here for the championship—in fact I feared I might never see her play again.

During those dark days of her illness, there was actually a time I feared Serena was going to die. The doctors said they could not rule that possibility out. She had blood clots in her heart that could be fatal. I didn't know what to think or what to do. Then, hope grew, but just as Serena started to recover, she got an infection in her stomach and had to have a drain tube put in to help her heal. This was after two surgeries on her foot and toe.

My children have been the center of my life since they were born, so I was beside myself with pain and fear. I never thought about tennis during those gloomy days. I just wanted my little girl to live. When you see someone you love more than anything in the world so close to death, especially your child, you'd willingly die to save her. All during the first matches of the tournament, it was unbelievable to me that we were here. Serena felt it, too. A few times before her early matches, she became a little shaky and nervous and I had to remind her of her confidence and about being a champion. I wrote a poem to her.

> *Step forward so you can see*
> *the light of day and know*
> *you are capable of*
> *conquering fear, defeating feelings of inadequacy,*
> *and rising above life's circumstances.*
> *One who is able to prevail*
> *is a shining example of*
> *power, strength, and confidence.*
> *It's just a matter of faith.*

I wanted Serena to understand that where she came from was great, where she was going would be terrific, but right now she should be elated just that she was here. I told her to forget about winning the tournament or losing the tournament.

"You go out there and you put your best foot forward," I told her. "Not the one you cut up—put the other foot forward." It made her laugh.

When Serena won the semifinal, I felt sure she would win the tournament. I didn't think anything could stop her now. Others were not so sure. I was walking the grounds before a tough match when a man said to me, "Your daughter could lose this next one, you know."

I said happily, "No, it's impossible. She can't lose."

"But it's such a tight match."

I waved that away. "That doesn't matter. It's impossible."

I knew he thought I meant "losing the match" was impossible. I didn't mean that at all. Serena couldn't lose a thing because just her being alive and here at all was a miracle. Everything else was small by comparison, immaterial. When Serena played Zheng Jie in the third round and the girl gave her such a hard time, I yelled out to Serena on the court, "Serena, relax and beat her like you did your sickness."

She looked at me with a twinkle in her eyes and went on to beat that girl.

When Serena got to the finals, she had such an easy victory in the first set I thought there was nothing to worry about. That's unusual. I'm like any other parent. I always worry. Even after all these years, it's terribly hard for me to watch my daughters play a match. But this one was going well. The first set was a blowout, 6–1. Then Serena faltered in the second and began making errors. Little by little, the set got away from her. She made small mistakes—a blown volley, a double fault, a down-the-line forehand long, and suddenly Agnieszka Radwańska broke her and evened the match at one set apiece.

I hate rain delays, but this one gave me an opportunity to go talk to Serena. Venus went with me. There is a special champion's area in the locker room but I couldn't go back there, so Serena came out. We all stood in the lobby near the polished wood staircase that leads up to the balcony where the champions greet the crowd after they've won. It didn't matter that there were tournament officials and members all around us, and thousands of fans outside.

"Serena, play her the same way I would play her, and you'll beat her," Venus told Serena.

Serena listens to Venus before she listens to anyone. Venus is not only her older sister, she's the assistant coach, maybe the whole coach. Venus meant "play her all out." Use your serve. Use your power. Think of yourself as a winner. Venus uses her big serve to pull her opponent wide and then blows her off the court with three or four strokes. She gave Serena a final hug and whispered, "There's nothing in the world that can stop you now."

That left just my daughter and me. Inside, I believed this Wimbledon final was going to be her greatest victory. I felt it with a sureness I could not explain. I got close to Serena and said, "You know you are a champion, and you know you can win. The three other girls you played before her, they couldn't beat you, and you're not gonna beat yourself here. You're representing life at this time, and it's your life. You know you're the best. Now, you go back out there and play to celebrate what life has given you."

She looked at me, smiled that smile, and said, "I will, Daddy."

I gave her a last hug and she went back to the locker room to prepare, and then back onto the court for the third set. Back in the box I kept saying, "Don't worry. Serena will win this match easily." Our family box was near enough to Radwańska's family that we could hear them yelling for their own girl. One of them said, "Can you believe how she's playing? She got a set on Serena. We could win this thing!"

I think some of the people in our box got a little worried. I tried to encourage them. It's the Williams way, my way, to take your trials and turn them into triumphs, to turn your contests into victories, to fight and never let anyone else define or defeat you. Down on the court, Serena looked up at me and smiled. I knew she had gotten the message. It was as if I could read her mind. *I beat this sickness, I can beat this girl,* and she did.

Serena won the championship and raced through the stands up to the box to hug me and her mother and sisters. I could not keep tears out of my eyes. I had brought two pairs of very dark sunglasses with me so no one would see if I cried. I gave that right up. I cried deeply when she won, but not because of her victory. Serena had survived death. She beat back all the evil forces of hell, stayed right here, and made this earth her heaven. I was so proud of her because I knew how hard she had fought to live, to give herself the opportunity to show how great she was once again.

All that and more I felt that morning so far from the place I was born and raised in Shreveport, Louisiana. Wimbledon, with its white rule and its traditions and its royalty, was the other end of the world. Yet, were things so very different? In tennis, just as in Shreveport, there was a crowd and I had often heard it grow ugly. I was never sure for whom it cheered. Many people said to me, "I'm not pulling against your daughter, we're just pulling for the underdog." It only reminded me how when we first came up, people pulled against us even when we *were* the underdog.

On that glorious morning of victory, the complexity of

life could not help but cross my mind. I was elated. I felt stature, unique. I felt like a young father, not my seventy years. Watching Serena race up to the family box, and every time she hugged me, I got a chill. My life had been so unique and special. Amidst the applause and cheers, I sat back for a moment and thought how blessed I was to have the two champions I predicted I would have, and how far we had come.

And because of that, I thought about Shreveport, where it all began . . .

CHAPTER **TWO**

Lightning almost stopped nineteen-year-old Julia Metcalf that stormy day in 1942, as she raced the old mule cart down the muddy dirt road. Jagged forked streaks tore across the big dark Louisiana sky and the thunder that followed pounded rain into her like a hammer. The labor pains were coming increasingly fast, spreading from deep within her swollen belly. She was thoroughly soaked, her clothes plastered to her body. She drove the mule harder. She had to get to Charity hospital, miles away. It was the only hospital close enough that would treat Negroes.

She flicked the reins harder. "Gettie up, Midnight."

She had first heard the distant thunder that meant a storm was coming earlier this cold and dark February day.

She grabbed the cardboard box she used to collect her wash from the clothesline and lit out back before it hit. Without warning, the first labor pains crashed through her body. She grabbed the clothesline for balance and struggled to stay on her feet. A second wave of pain hit but she continued to take her wash in, folding each piece carefully before placing it in the cardboard box.

A sharp pain hit her in the stomach. She dropped the box and fell to her knees with a shriek. Contraction subsiding, she picked up the laundry and made it into the old house. Puddles of rainwater had already formed on the floor. She was accustomed to leaks in the tin roof. She always put pots and tins beneath them to catch the water. Later, she would use it to wash clothes, or heat it on the stove for cooking or bathing. Rainwater was welcome in the house because it meant she wouldn't have to carry heavy buckets in from the well.

Julia's life had never been easy. Her father, Harold Metcalf, had been born to sharecroppers in 1895 in Natchitoches, Louisiana, just south of Shreveport. When he was twenty-one, he married Julia's mother, the former Julia Thompson, who had moved to Shreveport with her parents in 1914. They had four sons and four daughters, including Julia, who was named after her mother. The Metcalfs worked hard to make sure their children knew the word of prayer. Faithful believers, they put their trust in God and relied on him to fill their needs. Harold read the Bible aloud every night, and even as a baby, Julia liked best to climb up on her father's lap and read along with him. She was his favorite, maybe because she saw things differently than the other kids. When white people set Harold's barn on fire and it burnt to the ground, everyone screamed and cried. Not Julia. She just shrugged.

"Why y'all crying? Ain't nuthin' we can do about that barn.

It's gone and it ain't comin' back. We just have to help Daddy build another one. That's all."

Maybe, Julia thought as she ducked a tree branch swept by the wind, *that's why I was so calm when the pains first hit.* She had gasped as a stream of water burst from between her legs but just sat down in the rocking chair and rocked. She wasn't ready for the baby. She had no clothes, no diapers, nothing. Well, she thought, *she* wasn't ready, but the baby sure was, so she went to hitch up the mule without another word.

She drove the mule hard, feeling the rain hit her, ducking flying leaves and dirt from the cotton fields around her. Years before, after half a lifetime of picking cotton, her father had decided to quit and make his living as a sharecropper. He made a deal with a Mr. Richmond to work his fields, part of his earnings going to pay off his right to own the land outright. Harold did not know he was making a deal with the devil. After years of paying for the land, Harold assumed the land was rightfully his, and decided to go to Mr. Richmond to ask for the deed.

His wife was frightened. She begged him not to go. "If you make a big deal about it, they might tie you to a tree and whip the flesh off your back till you die."

A proud man, Harold's only response was, "I want what's mine."

Harold fought for composure as he went up to the big house. He held in his hand yellowed pieces of paper that showed each time he had made a payment, and for how much. The deal was he could buy the land for $150. Harold's records showed he had actually paid that sum off years before. He knocked on the big white door and a female house servant came and told him to wait outside while she fetched Mr. Richmond.

Mr. Richmond was very tall, over six feet, his black hair

streaked with gray. He had sharp eyes, one blue and one green, and a gaunt face with high hard cheekbones. He limped because his right leg was shorter than his left, and he wore boots with a special heel made to even it out. Mr. Richmond loved his black boots. They went all the way up to his knees. The boots were famous because he had a reputation for using them to kick Negroes in the head. He was proud of that. He used to tell people he could kick them in the head and the blood wouldn't even leave a stain.

"Mr. Richmond," Harold began, polite but firm, "I was wondrin' when you gonna give me the papers for my land. I done paid you all the money I owe you, suh."

Richmond's laugh held no humor. He looked Harold right in the eye and brought his face close. "Now, Harold. You know a nigger can't own land, don't you?"

Tears of anger and frustration welled up in Harold's eyes. He held up his papers. "But, suh, I paid you—"

Richmond cut him off. "My records show you still owe me fifty dollars. As soon as you pay me the rest of what you owe me, I'll be glad to give you those papers. Now, be a good boy and go back to the fields. We don't want to cause no hard feelings, do we?"

"No, suh."

"You been working for me too long for us to be enemies. I let your family live on my land for practically nothing and you come to me with some nonsense about *I* owe *you*? Get out of here before I have your black ass whipped to death."

"Yes, suh, Mr. Richmond. I didn't mean no harm. We still friends, suh?"

Mr. Richmond smiled a cold smile and slammed the door in Harold's face.

Harold was never the same after that. When he wasn't

working, or reading his Bible, all he talked about was leaving. "A man can't go round lettin' people cheat him. It ain't right. It just ain't right."

But he couldn't just ride off the Richmond land without a plan. It was surrounded by a fence, and both the front and back roads were blocked by gates. At night, Mr. Richmond put a lock and chain on them. When his family saw Harold was determined, fear set in. What if Mr. Richmond found out? What if he called the sheriff with his guns and dogs? But Harold would hear nothing about that. Every night he vowed to his wife, "Mama, I'll die before I stay on this land another day."

"But, Harold, we got a home and you just want to up and leave? That's crazy."

"We ain't got nuthin' and we don't own nuthin'. We don't even belong to ourselves. We belong to the white man. Now, I'm gonna take the children and go. If you don't come with us, we gonna leave you here."

It was dark the night the Metcalf family packed up to go. There was no moon, no stars, nothing to betray them. They took only what they could carry and headed for the back gate. The Metcalf farm was pretty far from the main house but the whole Richmond place was over twenty acres. Every sound startled the family. Every dog's bark seemed like it was meant for them. Two black men in field hand's garb were waiting with a wagon on the other side of the back gate. Harold and his family squeezed their belongings through a hole in the fence and the men helped them lift their few pieces of furniture over it and into the wagon. They helped the children over, too. They wanted to ride in the wagon but there was no room except for their mother.

The family walked for hours on dark and lonely roads. They jumped at every rustle in the woods. They knew they had to make a good distance because Mr. Richmond would be out looking for them as soon as he discovered they were gone, maybe as early as first light. They made it out of the county the first night and for several days moved from house to house, sheltered by other families, until they reached a community called Cedar Grove. There, Harold found a shack for the family and got some work . . .

"Ho, mule!" Julia shouted over the wind and rain, flicking the reins sharply. Torn from her reverie, she smiled grimly and wiped her wet face. What a sight she must be. All her life she was told what a beautiful woman she was, all smooth-skinned and bright-eyed, with a beautiful figure. Just look at her now. Belly swollen with child, hair matted and drenched, mouth clenched in pain. Well, everyone said her best feature was her kind heart. Maybe it was. Making friends was always easy for her. She got a lot of attention. But, she mused, not all of it was the right kind.

Well, her mother had warned her. "It don't make no difference you is innocent, girl. Lot of men gonna try and get you in bed anyhow."

Lightning forked across the sky again and thunder hit in rolling waves. The storm was all around her. Trees bent to the wind. The mule snorted and strained but kept on pulling. Cars passed her on the main road. It meant nothing. None of the white people would stop to help her or give her a ride even if they knew what pain she was in.

"Sorry, child. Niggers don't go in cars."

Julia almost screamed when the next pains hit. They were coming closer. She was almost to town. Where was the baby's father, R.D., when she needed him? She wiped her arms across her eyes to clear them and gave a bitter smile. Where he always was, gone.

She had first seen R.D. while she was walking home along the road by the river with her aunt Honey. He was fishing, but turned back to her and smiled a devilish smile.

She walked right past him.

"Mornin', Miss Julia. How are you today?" he called after her.

He was handsome, no doubt about that. And, Julia thought, he obviously loved to flash his fine teeth.

Her aunt had made no bones about her feelings. "That R.D. ain't up to no good. He don't hit a lick at a snake 'cause he think he too good to work in the field likes the rest of us. He call himself a music man but he just hang out in them jook joints drinking moonshine."

Curiously, that piqued Julia's interest. Her aunt continued, "I hear he can't play that old raggedy guitar worth a dime and he sure 'nuff can't sing. Don't let him catch his eye on you, little sister. People say he ain't got no place to call home. He just like to sleep around with a whole bunch of women and go from house to house!"

Julia remembered saying, "He look fine to me, Aunt Honey." And that was that.

Nobody had known when she first started seeing R.D. She was young and, well, sometimes passion got the best of people. She knew there were rumors they met in a barn at night. Soon, nothing was secret when she got pregnant with his baby. Her father was furious with her. He didn't think his favorite child could be out there having sex. Her sisters and brothers were angry, too. When the fights got too much, she moved into her own house. The family didn't make it easy for her. Even when she got real big, Julia still had to work in the fields and take care of other people's kids. There were no handouts. She had made her bed and had to lie in it, Daddy said firmly.

The wind whipped up suddenly and hit her like a slap. Julia fought the storm, driving the mule, not knowing where the rain ended and her tears started. She had to get help. She wasn't going to let this baby die. Pain distorted her features but she held on to the reins and surged Midnight forward. Suddenly, she felt a hard bump and Midnight began to slow. She yanked the reins harder but, abruptly, the old mule came to a complete stop and sank to the ground. He shook his head from side to side, an indication something was terribly wrong, and gave out an awful cry.

Julia got out of the wagon. Even in the driving rain, she could see the bump had been caused by a sinkhole in the road. Midnight had stepped in it the wrong way and broken his leg. She couldn't help him. She had her own pain to deal with. She pulled desperately at the reins while yelling, "Get up, you dumb mule. *Please* get up. I can't stay here. You gotta get up!"

Midnight didn't move. She cried because she knew it would take him time to die and she had no gun to put him out of his misery. She had to leave him there. She picked herself up and started down the road with the storm swirling all around her. Clutching her stomach, she stumbled forward, crying out, "Jehovah God, please, I need you right now." Between sobs, she kept saying, "I need you, Jesus. I need you, Jesus."

She made the main road and almost fell but managed to keep on going. Cars passed her and she knew the occupants could see her, but no one stopped. Then she saw the car of the white woman whom she worked for coming straight at her on the other side of the road. The relief was enormous. Julia waved her hand. The woman surely saw her. She had to see her, even in the rain. Julia felt her load lighten. Surely the woman would stop and help her.

The car slid by like a speedboat, throwing water in its tracks as it passed.

Julia kept on walking. It was still miles to the hospital. Streaks of lightning filled the sky. Thunder roared like an angry lion. When all hope was gone, she fell to her knees. She felt the warm seductive power of surrender come over her. *Just lie down and it will all be over. Let the pain go away. Let it all go away.* She couldn't. She got up. One step farther. One more step, and then another. All the white people in Louisiana could try to kill her but she wasn't going to let them. One more step, she told herself, and forced her feet to take it. Her baby wasn't going to die on this filthy road even if God sent all the lightning and thunder in the world down on her.

She prayed and she walked. One step farther. Then, another. When it was almost too much for her, she thought she saw a dim light in the distance coming toward her. Was it an illusion, born of desperation? Was it another white person who would pass her in his warm car? Under her breath she continued to pray, "I need you, Jesus. I need you, Jesus."

The light became brighter. It cast harsh shadows. Maybe it was the devil coming for her. She prayed for an angel. She never stopped praying. "I need you, Jesus. I need you."

An ancient rusty pickup truck coughing smoke from its exhaust rolled to a stop beside her and the old black man inside rolled down the window.

"Is that you, Julia? Do you need help?" He slid from the cab and kneeled beside her. "What are you doing out here, child? Some of those white fools could come along and rape and kill you."

Julia wiped her face in the rain and looked at him without a hint of recognition.

"Julia, it's Mr. Leroy. From church."

"I need to get to the hospital," she moaned.

"Oh, my Lordie, child. You out here in this rain trying to have that baby? Lord have mercy. Come on. I'll get you to the hospital."

Julia rose to her feet and Mr. Leroy helped her into the seat next to him. She was shivering uncontrollably, but the truck didn't have any heat. Mr. Leroy pulled off his coat and put it around her shoulders but it barely helped. She cried out, "I'm so cold."

Mr. Leroy reached down to the passenger floorboard of the truck and removed the blanket stuffed there to block the draft from the rust holes in the floor. He covered Julia as best he could and headed for the hospital. With the rain blasting against the windshield and the lightning flaring in the night sky, Julia laid her head back and fought the pain.

"Jehovah God, I need thee every hour and I need thee right now. Put your arms of protection around us so we can make it to the hospital, and then, Jehovah God, help me to have a healthy baby. Make my heart strong so I can live to raise my child. In Jesus' name, I pray. Amen."

The truck pulled up in front of the hospital. Mr. Leroy jumped out and ran around to help Julia out. He wrapped his arms around her and hurried her through the thick glass doors into the brightly lit hospital corridor. A nun came out from behind her desk and ran to them.

"Her baby's coming any minute," said Mr. Leroy, breathlessly. "You got to help her now."

Julia felt the world slipping away as the nun ushered her toward a delivery room. She turned and Mr. Leroy was still standing there, dripping water from his clothes onto the corridor floor, hat in his hands.

"Thank you, Mr. Leroy," Julia called back. "God bless you."

"And you, girl," he said. "And the baby . . ."

* * *

Julia Metcalf Williams gave birth to me, Richard Dove Williams, that night of February 14, 1942. The truth is, but for her strength, and the kindness of a stranger, my mother would have died that night and I would have died within her, left on the side of the road by depraved indifference, racism, and cruelty.

But we didn't die.

It is now more than seventy years later and I have walked a long road. I fought every hand raised against me in this world and raised my daughters to become the greatest female tennis players who ever lived.

I have survived my wounds and prospered mightily.

What follows is my story.

CHAPTER **THREE**

Growing up in Shreveport, Louisiana, you knew what everybody knew. Black boys were big, strong, and docile. Black girls were domestic and kind. Either way, we were expected to work in the cotton fields without question, reservation, or revolt. When I was a child, Negroes flocked to the fields like obedient puppies to perform mind-numbing chores. Conditioned to inequality by violence and a lack of education, we accepted racial disparity and learned to fake contentment in a hateful and segregated America.

The racial war in Shreveport in those days wasn't the only war going on. The Japanese bombed Pearl Harbor and America entered the war just two months before I was born. It seemed to me the entire world was fighting while I grew up.

World War II killed more people, cost more money, damaged more property, and affected the lives of more people than any other war in history. It also foreshadowed my own journey. Life was a battlefield, win or die.

Shreveport is located on the Red River in the northwestern part of Louisiana, three hundred miles northwest of New Orleans. In the 1940s, it was a quiet little city where everybody upheld the values of the times. That meant laid-back attitudes, obedient personalities, stagnant minds, and fearful hearts. Negroes in Shreveport were quarantined as if they had a contagious disease. To protect white folks, every facet of the city was segregated—restaurants, movie theaters, parks, hotels, and public accommodations. Negroes accepted it because whites had strategically subjugated their innate strength and character to keep them forever in darkness.

Blacks lived in a small area of the city in filthy, old, rundown houses near the railroad tracks, or in dirt road shanties in the woods. There wasn't much of a future in Shreveport. Too many young men got convicted of crimes, real or imaginary, and sent to the State Penitentiary at Angola. Too many more were lynched, burned alive, or beaten to death, their bodies tossed into the nearby Red River.

It was a terrible time. It was a terrible place. Young black girls had babies at an early age because white men raped them and then refused to acknowledge the crime, much less support them. My greatest fear was that one of my sisters would be raped, and I was always on the watch for their safety. Hatred fueled Shreveport. I often had to run from whites who tried to beat me up. I was chased with a stick, a bat, guns, and chains. My body has a lot of reminders of the violence I knew as a child. My nose was broken three times and my teeth were knocked out. I limp to this day because, as a child, I was stabbed in the leg with a railroad spike and an ice pick by members of the Ku Klux Klan.

One of the white men in the general store demanded I call him Mister and, when I refused, I had to fight him and three of his friends. Two of them wrestled me down and one hit me in the back of my head. I have a scar where he busted my skull open. It turned out to be a blessing, because I didn't feel any pain after that, not even when the fourth one jammed the railroad spike into my leg. I bled so much they must have thought they killed me, because they all got scared and took off.

My mother pulled the spike out when I got home. She told me, "It doesn't matter what happened. We all God's children."

I wasn't so certain.

In fact, as a child, I never understood why black people put their hope in God at all. We were taught to believe that one day, in the twinkling of an eye, God was going to come and take us to glory, where the streets were paved with gold. No more crying in the midnight hour, no more pain and suffering, no more disappointment, no more hatred, no more killings. I wasn't the smartest of children, but absolutely nothing in Shreveport led me to believe this was going to happen any time soon.

For that reason, it took a lot of courage, in that spring of 1942, for my mother, Julia Metcalf, a young Negro woman, to have me out of wedlock. Whites scorned her for her sin of fornication. Her own people compounded it by ostracizing her. The real problem was her messing around with R. D. Williams, my father, a man with a terrible reputation for living off women and having babies all over Shreveport.

R.D. was Mama's greatest weakness, the invisible man who impregnated her by night and disappeared from our lives by day. His "Harry Houdini" act eventually led to the birth of five children, four girls—Pat, Barbara, Penny, Faye—and me. I was the eldest, Richard Dove Williams, his only son.

I never understood my mother's attraction to my father. The world may now see me as a famous man in control of his destiny, but no one knows how much my early life defined me as a child, and later, as a husband and a father. Back then, it was customary to name a son after his father, so my mother did. As early as I remember, I hated my name because my father's love did not come with it. My name was a constant reminder of what I did not have and could not earn. It would always remind me of the man who left me alone, who abused my mother, and who put me way behind the starting line in the race of life.

As a child, I struggled to understand why my father didn't want me and why he didn't love me. Even now, those questions remain, and I am rarely comfortable with people, or within myself, regardless of the respect I have gained. When I was a child, my mother understood how much pain my father caused me and tried to make up for it. In the bedtime stories she read to me, she made sure I knew Richard was a king's name. She told me it meant "lionhearted." It took a long time for me to accept my name but I had to, to become what I believed I could be. I knew I would need a heart bigger than a lion's to make something of myself, a heart at least as big as the world that hated me.

My father publicly admitted I was his child but never made even the slightest effort to forge a bond between us. His presence in town was tantalizing—a father so near and yet so out of reach. As much as I tried to accept that, his rejection created a breach that would last for the rest of our lives. Yet, every child wants to love his father, and back then, I was no different. When I was in the third grade, I started pretending he lived with us. One rainy day after school, I stood in front of the building in the rain for over an hour, waiting for him to pick me up. He never came. After a while, my mom showed up carrying a homemade raincoat for me.

"Sonny, why are you standing here in the rain?"

"I'm waiting for my daddy to pick me up."

She touched my wet head tenderly. "He's not coming. Let's go home."

I struggled to love my father but grew to hate him even more as Mama continued to let him come over and make babies inside her. She used to say she was accustomed to a big family. After my last sister, Faye, was born, I confronted her.

"Mama, why do you let him keep doing that to you?"

She answered angrily, "That's not your business, Richard."

To me, it was. Something inside me needed to know why she allowed him to use her over and over again. I kept questioning her. Her response was always the same, her face turned away, curt and angry.

"It's not your business, Richard."

Every day of our life was a struggle to hold on to hope, a struggle to live. R.D. never got better. He never helped my mother or me or my sisters. It took a long while, but finally my mom saw that. One day when I questioned her, she seemed to take it more to heart, and answered sadly, "I don't know why I let him do that to me."

In time, she realized R.D. had no hope of ever changing. He didn't want us and we didn't need him. My mother was all the strength we needed, the backbone of our family. To this day, she is my greatest hero. She taught us the importance of sticking together. She created special bonds with each of us. As time went on, I began to treat the very idea of having a father as a figment of my imagination. He wasn't real. Neither was his love.

It's always been ironic to me that I was born on Valentine's Day, because for many years love was my most elusive quest. Throughout my life, I have tried to understand why it was so important to find someone to love me. My mother and sisters surely loved me, but I always felt something missing. It was something I would not find until I fathered my own children and had a family of my own.

That was when my life truly began.

There are many who think me a fierce, dominating, and controlling parent. Perhaps. Or perhaps I just know what it is like to grow up without a father's love and support and, in that, see the reason why being a husband and father has been the most important and all-encompassing role of my life.

Raising my children, fighting for them and protecting them, gave me the utmost love, pride, and satisfaction. Without doubt, of the many places I have been, and the many jobs I have done, the opportunity to be a good and loving father will always be my greatest joy and most solemn blessing.

CHAPTER **FOUR**

In Shreveport, my family and I lived in a three-room shack on East Seventy-Ninth Street, next to the railroad tracks. The house was so raggedy a strong wind could have blown it down. Outside, three uneven stone block steps led to the front door and the ripped screen door that squeaked every time it opened or closed. Countless leaks in the roof made it an indoor lake every time it rained.

The house was scarcely furnished. The front room had a woodstove and a fireplace. A sheet of plywood on top of four bricks was our version of a kitchen table. We used old crates in place of chairs. An old rocking chair occupied one corner with a kerosene lamp on top of a big pot next to it. In the other corner sat a fishing pole and a bucket.

The other two rooms were our bedrooms. Each room had a kerosene lamp on the floor and my mom hung blue-and-white flowered curtains over the windows. We did not have any beds. My mom made pallets on the floor from old quilts, blankets, and sheets, and we used cardboard boxes to store our clothes. We didn't have an indoor toilet, just an outhouse in the back-yard. One night, one of my uncles went to the outhouse and jumped up fast when he felt something touch his behind. A large black snake had crawled in through a hole in the siding. After that, we told Mama it was too scary to go out there so she kept a bucket next to the back door and we relieved ourselves in it. Every morning, I had to dump the bucket while the smell turned my stomach.

Our property was as raggly as the house. I thought our front yard was cursed because it refused to grow grass, but it did have the biggest tree I'd ever seen, with thick branches reaching out like twisted arms. Every afternoon, when Mama returned from the fields picking cotton, we used to sit in the shade under the tree and she'd rest. She came home with a rag or stocking on her head, so tired she could barely walk, unable to stand up straight from bending down all day. The heat was miserable. I don't know how she managed it. When I was an infant, she was all alone so she had to take me with her. She pulled me around those fields on top of her cotton sack, which was almost twelve feet long and could hold as much as two hundred pounds.

Despite her exhaustion, she always got herself and us kids ready for nightly prayer meetings at church. I secretly watched her groom herself. She could not afford makeup or body lo-tion, so she put cooking oil in her hair, and on her arms and legs. It was the saddest thing in the world to see, but at the same time the greatest act of love.

When she was ready, Mama led us down the road through the woods. She had no fear or reservation. She trusted the Lord would protect us. We attended the Church of Christ, a small wood-frame building that exploded regularly with the Holy Ghost. Prayer warriors chanted in uninterpretable language and tongues. Women filled with the spirit ran up and down the aisles while others fainted and foamed at the mouth.

Reverend Bullard, a short, fat, baldheaded man with big bulging eyes and a big bass voice, shook the building as he intoned, "Father, I stretch my hand to thee, no other help I know. If thou should draw thyself from me, tell me where shall I go?"

The congregation repeated the hymn in perfect unison. Prayers were a direct plea to God. Without Him, where would we Negroes be? Without God's protection, wouldn't our lives be much worse? I sat there silently as the congregation sang the words and then began to hum and moan because, they said, that way the devil didn't know what we were talking about.

The service lasted until the moon rose. We all filed out and I took my mom's hand as she said good night to the reverend and the choir and her friends. Once outside, all that chanting and testifying faded into silence and the sounds of the forest were like a soft blanket as we stole into the night with my hand in hers, walking quietly back home.

My mom, actually, was never supposed to have kids. She was born with a hole in her heart. The doctor told her if she got pregnant, she would probably lose the child before full term. Mama always smiled and shrugged off the doctor's warnings. Her philosophy was simple. "If you believe things will go wrong in your life, they will—if you believe they'll go right, they will."

For me, the verdict on that philosophy was in doubt. I

doubted it even further when she sent me downtown to the market called Peoples, to get a soup bone. A soup bone is one that the butcher has cut all the meat off and sells to poor people to make soup. It was unusual for my mom to want one. She mostly cooked things grown in the ground. We always had grains, beans, okra, and a lot of good turnips and carrots. But today, she wanted a soup bone.

I walked down to the market and was having a good time, being a kid, pushing the basket down the aisles when I accidentally bumped into a white lady.

"Nigger, can't you see where you're goin'?" she fumed. "You ain't got no business drivin' that thing like that."

I was in trouble. I had been noticed. A couple of white boys nudged each other and sidled outside. They'd be waiting for me. I mumbled something to the white lady and walked away. The bone I got from the butcher barely had a strip of meat on it. I told him I didn't want him to wrap it. I wanted to carry it in my hand.

The biggest boy was waiting when I came up to the checkout. "Nigger, what did you buy?"

"A soup bone," I told him.

"Well, I'm takin' yo' damn bone after you pay for it," he said.

I said, "And I'm gonna give it to you, too."

When he reached his hand into his pocket for a knife, or whatever was in there, I hit him as hard as I could with that big bone. Bones like that have knots on the end where they fit into joints, and I caught him right on the side of the head. The knot almost took his eye out. He grabbed his face, bleeding, and I ran off as fast as I could, losing the bone in the process.

I thought I had won, but I just couldn't escape a beating

that day. Mom walloped me because I came back without the bone and I couldn't tell her why. She already thought I had too much hatred in me. It was a constant theme in our discussions. She made me read the Bible and told me how important it was to have God in your life. She told me I had to be peaceful and tolerant.

I asked her, "But, Mama, aren't *you* prejudiced?"

She nodded. "Absolutely."

I smiled. Here was proof I was right in my thinking.

"Sonny, I *am* prejudiced—against you."

I was shocked. "Me? Why?"

"Just look at you. You're raggly. You don't have anything. If I don't buy you no clothes you'd be naked, wouldn't you? Sonny, you don't have nothin'. Your bicycle is out there broken down with a flat. You don't have no get-up or ambition. Sonny, you don't try to do much with your life, do you? In fact, you're not doin' anything."

To teach me about life, since I had no real father, she began looking around for a male figure to guide me. I was already working on East Seventieth Street for Dr. Carter, a white man who hired me to sweep out his office every day before school. I made a dollar and a half a month. On one occasion, he scolded me for not doing a good job. I resented it and told Mama, "I'm not going to the doctor's office anymore."

She looked angry. "You're not gonna be the same way he be about you, son. You can't. Now, let's go see him."

There was no arguing with my mother, so we went. When we got there, Mom asked him to come out, and when he did, she pointed to me.

"Doc, whatever you said to my son you did the right thing. You know this boy don't have no daddy."

He looked at us over his spectacles. "Yes, ma'am."

"Well, from this day on, *you're* his daddy and we're gonna bring him up together."

I thought both of them were crazy. They must both hate me. I soon came to realize that Dr. Carter and my mom had more knowledge than I ever knew. Dr. Carter did a lot to help me. He let me work for him and put money aside for me. He was a good man, a kind soul. If I complained to Mama again about his being prejudiced, she'd say, "Sonny, no one's in the world prejudiced unless you see prejudice. And if you see prejudice, it just means you have to do a little bit more work to free your mind from it."

It was one of the biggest lessons in my life. Mama wouldn't allow me to see prejudice. Under no circumstance could I walk in and say, "Mama, that Jewish guy's prejudiced," or "That white guy's prejudiced. That Mexican there, he ain't' no good. He's prejudiced." She wouldn't hear of it. It took me a long time to understand what she was trying to teach me—that every person had a responsibility to make something of himself no matter how people saw him. What you find in life, you deal with. If everybody hates you, *tough*. If everybody says you can't do something, *tough*. If you refuse to be beaten, you *won't* be. If you gave in, you were just cooperating with whoever was trying to stop you. What did that mean to my life? It meant racism could never be an excuse for anything.

Of course, Mama clearly knew racism was there. It wasn't like it escaped her in the cotton fields. She just would not allow me to hide behind it. We got on a bus once, and there was a guy taking up two seats. When he saw me coming, he got on the outside seat and said, "I can't move my legs, can you sit somewhere else?"

I got hot. "You're gonna move over so my mom can sit down."

He did, but when we got home, Mama asked me, "Why was it so important to you that I sit down?"

I said, "Mom, you don't have to stand if there's an extra seat there."

She smiled at me, and these were her exact words: "Son, you're gonna be a great man when you grow up. God is all inside of you. Now, I don't know what else is inside, but don't you worry about that 'cause you can't take a good man and hold him down and you can't take a bad one and prop him up. I don't know how you got to be the way you are, but I know you are going to tear up this world and be just fine, no matter what they throw at you."

My mom died in 1985. Three days before she passed, I came back to Shreveport to make sure she had everything she needed. She was lying in bed with her medications beside her on the bedstand. She had lived a long life and she was tired, but her smile said everything about the hope and dreams she had seen realized in her children and grandchildren. As I was about to leave, I saw a man walk through the house wearing a white suit. He was only there for an instant, then gone.

"Mama, who was that man walking in your house?" I asked her.

"What man?"

"Mama, I just saw a man walk through here."

"What did he have on, Sonny?"

"He had on all white clothes."

She smiled contentedly. "Sonny, that's my angel come to take me. God sent him. I won't be here much longer now."

Three days later, she was gone.

Some years after she passed, vandals desecrated her cemetery, scattering the headstones. My sisters feared we could not locate Mama's grave. I was getting ready to go and hurt someone, but I thought about what Mom would say. Instead, I checked things out and got my sisters together. I explained to them that when they bury a person, the grave is recorded on a map. That calmed them, and the headstone was soon replaced. But I needed more. For me to be sure, I had to dig up the grave itself. I had buried three things with her on the day of her funeral that would identify her grave to me more certainly than any map.

I took a shovel from her garage, dug down three or four feet, and found what I had buried. I had put those things there to make sure she had a part of me with her always. I will never tell anyone what these things were, but it was a great relief to find them.

My mom is still my greatest hero. Without the love she planted in me, I believe I'd probably be dead, or in jail, because with all that I have lived through, I believe the rage that lived in me would have made me kill someone. My mom was the first one to see that the best in me was yet to come. She always told me God had something very special for me and she prayed to Him and asked him to open my eyes so I could see it.

I never have seen it.

I am still looking.

CHAPTER **FIVE**

I have learned a thing or two about people who accomplish great things. They never see themselves as great. When I read all the "great" things I do, the things that make the newspapers or television, it's amazing to me anyone believes it's special. I don't see it. I am nothing special. Maybe that's why I realized at a very early age that any success I had in life would come from hard work. I can't say I phrased it exactly like that, but I knew I had to do things myself. It started with getting a job. A job was not an option; it was a necessity. At five, I started sweeping Dr. Carter's office. At eight, I cleaned the bottom of oil tanks after school. At nine, I went to work for the Louisiana Fence Company.

Everyone at the fence company worked as a team out on the

road and in the fields. The lowest guy dug dry holes. The next poured in cement, the last put the fence post in and wrapped a tie-wire around the crossbeam to hold it all together. Of course, I dug holes. It was hot and boring work. Worse, times were getting even tighter in my family as R.D. added more kids to it.

I wanted to work up to the tie-wire position, which was easier and paid better. I thought, *You don't fail by trying—you fail by not trying.* So I asked the boss for the promotion. He looked at me like I was crazy.

"You're too young. We want someone older."

To this day, I am not sure where I found the inspiration to say, "Boss, I'm old enough. I'm married and have two kids."

His forehead creased like I had just told him I could fly. "Boy, you have to be joking."

"It's not a joke, boss."

"Yeah? Let me see 'em," he challenged me.

I knew a girl who had two brothers much younger than she was, so I told her to tell the little ones to call me Daddy, and took them all down to the job site. When the boss saw me, he sat back on his heels and gave a huge grin.

"Well I'll be damned," he said. "You niggers do anything, huh?"

He saw what he believed. I used to laugh to myself as he went around telling people, "You know that damned boy, you won't believe it. He has two kids. I've seen them." Any white men came on the site, he'd call them over and point, grinning. "Hey, boys, this damn monkey do have some children."

I got the job with the better money and got called "monkey" from then on. In some ways, it was kind of a badge of honor, because if you look at the monkeys, or bears, or any animal you can think of, they take care of their family—except for my dad, that is. Respecting yourself and taking care of your responsibilities, no matter how young you were, was the way my mother brought me up. It was also how I brought up Venus and Serena.

The most important thing to teach children is to have respect for themselves, because no one is ever going to respect you unless you do. My kids were educated at an early age and learned to work at an early age. They were taught to love themselves so they would have the confidence to make good decisions and strong commitments. If a person doesn't make a real commitment, he will never succeed. I surely don't understand all these parents today who are always telling their kids how special they are, without them proving it. That's not faith, it's flattery.

Looking back, I suppose my life back then was somewhat of a contradiction. In the worst of environments, I had the best of upbringings. When the world tried to teach me I was nothing, less than nothing, someone who could be stolen from, I developed a self-worth that was untouchable. When my father never gave anything to me, I decided I was going to give my family everything I had.

The more I worked, the more I helped Mama and my sisters, and the prouder of myself I became.

"Mama, I'm the man of the house now, right?" I asked her one day.

She laughed. "How can you be the man of the house when you're only a child yourself?"

"Mama, I work three jobs to take care of us. When I get paid, I bring all my money home to you. We don't need R.D. anymore, do we?"

Mama just stared out the window. I was angry because I wanted to be the man of the house so badly. Then she turned back and took my face in her hands. I can still see the hurt in her eyes and the flow of tears as she spoke.

"Richard, from this day forward you are the man of this house and R.D. won't come round here no more."

I hugged her so tight I almost suffocated her.

The money I brought home barely made ends meet but we survived. I used to go out in the woods and hunt bullfrogs to eat, and fish, and shoot rabbits, and steal chickens. We didn't have a refrigerator. We had an icebox and used fifty-pound blocks of ice from the iceman. One day, I bought some meat from the market and found maggots in it. It was winter and we were so hungry I could not force myself to throw it away. I cooked it, maggots and all. It wasn't the first time we ate tainted or spoiled meat. We couldn't throw anything away, not even bad meat.

Caring for my family as best I could was where I first learned to be a father. My sisters were easy to grow up with and I think they were pleased by what I did for them. I made little carts and pushed the girls up and down the street in them. My sisters loved holidays, especially Christmas, and they believed in Santa Claus. Mama used to buy them bikes as presents from a store named Auto-Lite on East Seventieth Street, but she couldn't afford them for all four. Helping Mama make their holiday perfect was my goal. For Christmas, I bought old bikes, spray-painted them, and put on new tires and rims so they looked brand new.

Personally, I didn't celebrate Christmas or believe in Santa Claus. Mama tried to convince me otherwise, but I was adamant. It didn't make sense to me why any white man would take a night out of the year to bring us gifts. Anyway, what did it matter if a man masked himself in religion one day and the next wore the white hood? One Christmas, I saw a white Santa Claus sitting in a department store inviting all the little white children to sit on his lap and share their Christmas list.

"Hop up here and sit on old Santa's lap. What do you want for Christmas, pretty girl?"

The girl giggled and said, "A baby doll."

Santa said, "Make sure you listen to your mama and daddy 'cause Santa knows if you been good or bad."

The little girl gave him a big hug. He pinched her rosy cheek and she ran into her mother's arms. He seemed so nice and kind, I decided to sit on his lap, too.

When I got to him, he said, "You better get your little nigger ass away from me, boy."

By the time I was eight, Mama gave up and stopped buying me Christmas gifts. She also gave up trying to talk me into embracing a holiday created by and for white people. White people bought things for each other. White families celebrated warm and happy and full of good food. White store proprietors benefited because sales increased and profits soared.

The truth wasn't lost on me, even at that young age.

When the turkey, stuffing, cakes, and pies were gone, we were still poor.

I thought my mother was a genius when it came to most things. When it came to how to get through life, I thought she was one of the most wrong-thinking persons I ever met. I suppose it couldn't have been otherwise. She grew up in very different times. She couldn't think differently. The idea of freedom never came her way. She just learned how to be the way she was and just accepted it.

My boyhood was a series of lessons in life. When I was little, I bought a piece of candy at the general store and when I went to pay for it, my hand accidentally touched the white owner's hand. It was a solemn rule that black kids were supposed to put their money on the counter. He snarled at me, "Don't you ever put your goddamn hands on me, boy. I hear that color of yours'll wear off and I damn sure don't wanna be a black-ass nigger like you."

"Excuse me, sir," I said, going through the subservient motions of bowing my head and lowering my eyes. From out of nowhere, a stick crashed across my back. I doubled over just in time to miss another blow. Severely shaken, I stumbled home like the drunks I'd seen, thinking bitterly all the way, *They ain't got no right to treat me this way. They ain't got no right. I'm somebody, too.*

It didn't take long for me to realize that Mama's accepting model of life was not for me. But where does a black child in the slums of Shreveport find a new model? Where does he find successful people to copy? Very few folks where I came from, if any, were successful, but there were some. I watched and wrote little notes and made little comments to myself. I tried to associate with people who were good role models. Mr. Macey was the manager of the A&P. I thought maybe I should be exactly like him because he was successful. Based on Mr. Macey, successful people had bald heads, big stomachs, and were extremely polite. But even he taught me something. He used to say, "Richard, success is nothing more than taking advantage of every opportunity."

Mr. Macey was right. He had confidence. He had faith in himself. If I wanted to be confident, I'd have to have faith in *my*self. That became my first principle: To be confident, you had to have faith. But faith in what? Some of the black people I knew in Shreveport believed maybe you could be a preacher, a teacher, or work in a factory—but the number-one job was picking cotton. I had made my mind up long before that I was not going to pick cotton. I didn't see one cotton picker or laborer that was successful at anything. So I tried to learn to do little things to build my faith, like seeing if I could walk down to East Seventieth Street, where there was a market, in ten minutes. When I could do that, I had set a goal and achieved it. I could have faith. A light went on in my head. Goals could be achievements. I had started the process of gaining faith in myself.

As a child, it was a great lesson that the process of setting and attaining a goal lets you gain faith in yourself. I kept it up. I learned how long I could run at top speed. I learned how far top speed would take me. I learned the time it would take for me to reach the woods where I could hide in safety if white people got behind me to beat me or kill me. I needed to run at top speed for nine minutes.

Soon, I learned that I had to be able to do better than that, because I almost got killed running only nine minutes. I was coming from downtown Shreveport and a white guy asked me, "Hey, aren't you the kid that said something back to my wife? You called her by her first name, is that right?"

"Yes, that's right," I said.

"Well, haven't you been trained to call her by her last name? Don't you know you got to call her Mrs. or Miss?"

I said, "I don't call no one that."

He pulled out a knife and two or three of his buddies got behind me. I took off. I knew I could outrun them if I could make nine minutes. They would fall behind. What I didn't realize was, they had a car. How dumb was I? In the nine minutes it took me to get to the area of safety, driving, they made it in four. They were waiting for me when I got there. What do you do when you've run at top speed and you get to the end and need more? I learned that fear can be a great incentive. When they came at me with bottles and knives, I ran until my heart was going to burst and the wind made my eyes tear from running so fast.

FEAR CAN BE A POWERFUL MOTIVATION became another rule of mine. From that day on, fear made me train myself to be able to run as fast and as long as I needed to run to survive. Fear of failure is a great motivation, too, especially if it's linked to survival. I learned that to reach your best, sometimes you have to be scared, especially of failing. Fear works two ways. You may know who *you* fear. Sometimes, however, to win, you have to do something to make people fear *you*.

By the time I was seven or eight, I got sort of known for running. One time, in a store, a white kid said to me, surprised, "I can't catch you."

I said, "No, you can't catch me."

He smiled and his lips curled meanly. "But I will," he said.

If you look closely at the back of my head on the left side, there's a scar where he snuck up behind me and hit me in the head with a bottle. I heard people say, "Boy, he's bleedin' like a ho." It didn't matter. All I knew was I had to run—and if I could get ahead of him, he wasn't going to catch me unless he was in a helicopter.

Fear creates theories. THEORIES MUST BE TESTED. That's another rule. Every time he or the other white kids saw me, an incident would start all over again. So I came up with a new theory. They knew I was scared of them, so maybe the only way for me to stop them was to make them scared of *me*. I made a slingshot and when they started up with me, I shot them.

As they ran, I heard them say, "That nigger is crazy!"

It helped me a great deal. It restored my faith. They stayed away from me. But, as I say, theories must be tested. Kids learn a lot that way and parents should always remember it. My theory of retaliation worked just fine until they brought something more powerful than a slingshot. It's called a rifle. They didn't mind shooting you down there in Louisiana, and I got shot at quite a few times till I learned that my best bet was to stay far away from people I was not going to call Mr. or Mrs.

Test your theories. You will live longer.

I perfected my plans and my running, and the next fight I got in, to escape from the white guys who were after me, I ran from downtown Shreveport to my house, maybe six miles away. The running part didn't bother me. I could now run fifteen miles or more easily. But I knew I'd have a problem ducking and dodging them this near to my house and, in the end, maybe lead them to where my family lived.

I veered off into the forest. At that moment, you would have seen me grinning. It wasn't *me* who had a problem. Now *they* had the problem. I had a lot of hate in me in those days. No matter what Mama said, or what I was taught in school or church, I felt I was doing the right thing to fight back—to fight any way I could. By now, I could see the forest trees and hear the branches swept by the wind. I was the happiest human being in the world because I knew they were in deep trouble. They sure were.

Once I got into the woods, I led them into the dry undergrowth. With the wind blowing and them chasing, I set the woods on fire. I knew all the ways out, but they didn't. I didn't care. If they'd gotten trapped in there I would have been happy. They weren't going to take a bottle to my head, or catch and beat me, not if they were running from being burned alive.

I think those people got out of the woods, but I left before I found out. When I got home, I sure couldn't tell Mom what I did, because she had already told me how she felt about my anger at white people. It just would have convinced her I was going to hell for sure.

Unfortunately, subsequent events did convince her.

We were living on East Seventy-Seventh Street in the Cedar Grove section. To cross Seventy-Seventh at Fairfield Avenue, you had to walk past houses where white people lived. Lots of them had dogs, and if you walked past on the street, the owners turned the dogs loose to bite you. Sometimes, they'd wait for a black woman or a child to pass, then release the dogs from houses in front and behind, so there was no place to run when they charged.

They caught me good that day, walking down the street. Maybe I should have tried to run, but I was suddenly in between four or five dogs barking and nipping at me and wanting to bite the living hell out of me. For all my theories, even as fast as I was, I wasn't going to outrun them. I had to stand my ground. I pulled out my slingshot and hit one or two and that backed them up for a moment. With nowhere to hide, I leaped up onto the front porch and crashed in through the front door. In those days, white people kept their guns in trophy cases or over the fireplace. I knew this because I had broken into lots of houses to steal things. Could I have gotten out the back and escaped? Maybe. But I had too much rage, too much fury, to back down. My blood was hot, my heart was pumping, and the one thing I knew for sure was that I had not done a damn thing to deserve being bitten by dogs.

I found a .22 caliber rifle and a .410 shotgun, both loaded. The dogs were still barking and snarling outside. I went through the front door and started shooting. I laid two dogs to rest, squealing, and I was just as ready to kill the others. They were coon dogs. They didn't have sense enough to back off. I hit one with the .22 and he went down. The only reason I didn't kill them all was a black lady named Sugar Doo, who lived near the corner of Fairfield, saw the commotion and yelled at me, "Child, I'm gonna tell your mama!"

I threw the guns down and ran off.

I hid for a while. The owners of the dogs called the police, but by that time, the local officer, Dale Baker, wouldn't come get me. He thought I was a crazy nigger and I would just as soon kill him if he tried to take me to jail. That was more and more my attitude. The older I got, the more I was starting to live to die. I was like a lot of the black kids in gangs I saw, years later, when I lived in Compton.

When my mother found out what I'd done to the dogs, she shook her head sadly and told me, "You think those people are prejudiced? Richard, you just a kid but you the most prejudiced human being I ever met." She walked away, shaking her head. "Sonny, you got more hatred in you than any child I've ever seen."

I wanted to talk back and say, "Mama, what would you have done?" But I couldn't backtalk her. Besides, I knew the answer. She would have accepted it. That did not make sense to me then, and still doesn't, but I got what she was trying to teach me. Avoid things and you don't have a problem. The way to survive was to live a life of evasion. You didn't get into conflict. You didn't pass by the house where you knew dogs lived. You kept to your own. You backed down. You were subservient.

That was what she desired for me, but I just could never be that way.

See, all I could think of was what would have happened if Mama or my sisters had been walking past those houses when the white people set their dogs on them.

It made me smile.

The dogs wouldn't bother them now.

CHAPTER **SIX**

When it came to school, Mama started me out right. I learned my numbers and ABCs before I ever went. When I was very young, she would say a letter, then make me repeat it. Sometimes, I would have to stand in our front room for over an hour saying the ABCs.

At two, it was not easy to hold my attention. "Be still, Richard, and say your letters," Mama chided.

By the time I was four, my mom would say the letter and I had to point to an object that began with the same letter. If I didn't match the letter to the right object, Mama would hit my legs with a switch till they were on fire. I'd fidget from the pain.

"Boy, be still and listen. You got to learn to listen if you want to get anywhere in this world. Do you hear me, son?"

"Yes, ma'am."

"You got to learn so you can teach your sisters. I don't want no ignorant children."

"Yes, ma'am."

Mama was a great woman, and her smile lit up the room. An optimist, she always had something positive to say about people. She was kindhearted and loving, and would do anything to help anyone. She used to say, "I don't know nothin' bad 'bout nobody. The Lord giveth and the Lord taketh away. Ain't no need for me to be selfish with people who in need, 'cause whatever I got, God gave me that."

Mama did not have any college degrees, but she had a Ph.D. in the psychology of life. Rarely giving me a direct answer to a question, she preferred to make me think things through on my own. Today, parents do everything for their kids. Ask a question; get an answer. Look how smart Daddy and Mommy are. My mama wanted me to discover reason and understanding on my own. She had an unyielding determination that all of her children would be able to confront life on their own terms.

I can't say Mama had specific aspirations for me. Being a lawyer or a businessman was an unrealistic dream back then. My mom simply believed that in order to be anything, you had to get an education. She would line us up and take us to the cotton field and we'd stand there for what seemed like an eternity.

Finally, she'd ask, "What y'all see?"

Being the oldest, I answered first. "I just see a whole lotta cotton, Mama."

"You ain't lookin' deep enough," she said. "What I see is work that ain't gonna take us nowhere. All I see is aches and pain. All I see is white, the white man's cotton, the white man's land, the white man's house, the white man's money. You get your lessons like I tell ya to, and one day you ain't gon' have to work in no cotton field. You hear me?"

"Yes, ma'am," I said, and I surely did.

By the time I was five, Mama had taught me the ABCs, numbers, colors, and how to write my name. After years of looking over her shoulder while she read the Bible, I was also a very good reader. We always read the Bible. It was the only book we had, because Negroes weren't allowed to go to the library and check out books.

There was no kindergarten in those days, so I started school in the first grade. The name of the school was Little Hope, located on Seventy-Third and Line Avenue. The name was absolutely correct. Negroes had little hope there. With its ancient wooden frame and tin roof, Little Hope was just like the run-down row houses of our neighborhood. The school couldn't afford a flagpole, so there was just a tired old American flag nailed to a long stick that was bolted to the tin roof. The other kids were proud to see the flag waving in the wind. I wondered how they could embrace such foolishness. Why did we clothe ourselves in the flag of patriotism and celebrate democracy when the chains of hatred and segregation bound us? Why did we put our faith in a world that was clearly out to kill us?

Failing to see what others saw in the flag, I came up with my own color scheme. Red, white, and blue painted a sordid picture. White represented evil intent and racial superiority. Red represented the shedding of innocent blood. Blue represented the senseless murders of my people. The truth could not be hidden behind a colorful rainbow.

Robbed of our heritage, we had no identity. We were just *niggers*, unlearned, unintelligent, and without hope.

Our school reflected my "color" scheme. Most of the windows were broken, with the panes filled in with cardboard. There were no air conditioners or heaters. In the summertime, we sweltered. In the winter, we froze. School started in September, an extremely hot month. To endure the heat, we sat in the playground under a shade tree. One water fountain trickled out a thin stream. Everyone would gather around and drink like thirsty animals despite the green slime and bird droppings covering it. There was one filthy outdoor bathroom. It was common to find maggots on the floor.

It was totally unsanitary. There was no place to wash our hands or faces after we came in from the playground, where we ate, too. Without a cafeteria, we all brought lunch. Mine was most often a piece of leftover cornbread. I'd forget it was in my pocket, so it usually turned into crumbs. The only saving grace was a one-room shack we called "the nickel lady's house," across from the schoolyard on Line Avenue, where kids who were fortunate enough to have a nickel or a dime could buy snacks.

Unlike the kids of today, no one made a fashion statement at my school. Boys wore dry-rotted shirts, and pants with holes in the knees. Girls' hems hung from under their dresses. I never worried about being outdressed by the other kids. We all wore the same clothes every day and were all just as poor. No one had athletic shoes. We wore our Sunday-go-to-meeting shoes, the only ones we had. When we took them off to play, piles of patent-leather shoes and work boots sat in the dirt in the middle of the playground.

Shoes were the most difficult article of clothing to keep in good repair, because we kept outgrowing them and were too poor to buy new ones. Kids came to school with holes in their shoes, or no shoes at all. When I didn't have any more shoes, I decided to make me a pair. I looked through the trash and found a pair of matching soles. I poked holes around the edges of each and ran fishing wire through the holes, knotting the ends so they couldn't come out. Wrapping rags around my feet for socks, I stepped on top of the soles and pulled the fishing wire together over them. I twisted the wires together with pliers until the soles stayed on my feet when I walked. It was a creative but painful experience. All the kids admired my fancy shoes when I went to school, but as the day went on, the fishing wire slowly cut into me. Stubborn as ever, I refused to take off my new shoes. By the time I got home, my feet were swollen and bloody.

The next day I was back to barefoot.

My first-grade teacher's name was Mrs. Williams, no relation to me, a small, fragile woman who looked too old to be working. There were more than forty children in our class, from six to fourteen. Mrs. Williams didn't have a roll book so she scribbled our names in the back of her Bible. I was surprised she didn't run out of room to write.

Mrs. Williams was a dedicated teacher and made the best of things. We were too poor to buy school supplies so she brought pencils, tablets, and bags of rocks from home. There were no desks, so we sat on old wooden chairs and held our tablets in our laps. We didn't have books, so she wrote our lessons on the chalkboard and divided the class into two groups. One group worked on counting, using the rocks. The other copied lessons from the board.

Mrs. Williams made a lasting impression on me. Married to a preacher, she insisted we start each day with a prayer. Her prayers were so strong I felt like God himself was present in the room. I behaved, because I feared she would send the Holy Ghost after me. On the other hand, the principal, Mr. Green, was a stumbling drunk who did nothing to fix the school's run-down condition. I hated how his breath smelled of alcohol whenever he walked by and patted me on my back. I used to see him behind the school drinking from a bottle in a brown bag. I also saw him passed out in an alley one weekend, only to reappear at school Monday morning in a badly wrinkled suit, his tired red eyes indicating his habit.

My fondest memory of first grade was meeting my best friend, Chili Bowl. He was just as poor as I was, and wore the same pair of overalls and suspenders every day, just like me. He never brought lunch, or had any money, so we shared what I had. He had an infectious smile and loved to play, but what fascinated me most about Chili Bowl was his thirst for learning. He was always trying to find a book to read to make himself smarter.

One day I asked him, "Chili Bowl, why you always lookin' for somethin' to read?"

"So I can get a good job when I grow up," he answered. "My hands hurt when I pick cotton with my mama in the field."

Chili Bowl was eight years old, the oldest of seven children. He was two years older than I was, but in the same first grade as me because he started late. His mother was always pregnant with another baby. People called his six brothers and sisters "side-steppers" because of their ages—six, five, four, three, two, and one.

Chili Bowl was in the same boat as me—he didn't have a father. Curious about how his family worked, I walked Chili Bowl home one time. His house looked all raggly and spooky, so I asked, "Chili Bowl, do you see haints at night?" A "haint" was what we called a ghost or spirit.

"Ain't no haints in my house," he spat angrily.

I wasn't so sure. The front yard was all scraggly weeds. In

back, drying wash danced on the clothesline as a small black dog jumped and barked underneath, trying to snatch things. Nevertheless, a delicious smell flowed out the back door and caught my nose. Chili Bowl's mother was cooking. She was young but looked very tired, and came out as we climbed the rickety stairs.

She said, "Richard, your mama know you over here?"

"Yes, ma'am," I replied.

"Okay, but make sure you get your butt home 'fore dark," she warned.

I nodded firmly. Believe me, the presence of haints assured it.

Once, Chili Bowl told me he was spanked because he broke a spoon. He had been digging holes in the yard and the spoon bent and broke. His mother slapped him upside his head and said, "I ain't got no money to buy no spoon. What we gon' eat with?"

He told me they had one spoon, one fork, and one knife. The family shared them at dinnertime. Sometimes, he had to eat with his hands. I wondered how they made it. The bedroom he shared with sisters and brothers didn't have any furniture. The only thing in the room was a sheet filled with cotton. They used it as a mattress.

I had thought my family was surely the poorest family on our street, the poorest in the Cedar Grove community where we lived, and, without a doubt, the poorest in Shreveport. It came as a surprise to me that we weren't actually the poorest family in town. At least we had forks and knives when we ate.

School was tough for me until I met Chili Bowl. Before he was there to protect me, I got into lots of fights. The older kids picked on me—especially about the size of my nose. I hated it. Chili Bowl made school much better. He protected me. My enemies were his enemies. He was so tough, even the older kids didn't pick on me when Chili Bowl was around. It was a nice feeling.

After school, Chili Bowl and I would lie in the yard with our hands behind our heads, gazing toward the sky with twigs hanging from our mouths, a manly pose. We talked about all the things we wanted to do when we grew up.

"I wanna move away from here one day," Chili said seriously. "I'm gon' get me a good job, a fancy car, a big house, and have lots of money. I ain't gon' be pickin' no cotton for nobody. I'm gon' make somethin' outta myself, Richard, you watch and see."

Out of the blue, I asked, "You think God hears us when we pray?"

Chili Bowl hesitated. "My mama say he'll answer all of our prayers, but so far he ain't answered none of mine. We still poor."

I laughed and got up and yelled at the sky. "God, do you hear us down here?" I picked up a stick and started banging on an empty can from the garbage, yelling at the top of my lungs, "God, are You up? God? God, are You up?"

Chili Bowl scowled. "What you doin' that for?"

Laughing, I answered, "I'm trying to wake God up. He must be sleeping 'cause He ain't answered none of my prayers, either."

Chili Bowl and I had a lot in common—we both had nothing. To make some money, Chili Bowl redeemed empty pop bottles for their two-cent-each deposit. We decided to work together to gather and sell more bottles to save enough money to start a business, even though we had no idea how to start one. Our plan was to sell enough bottles to buy a foot-tub to harvest local fruit. Berries and plums were plentiful and we could pick and sell them.

Early the next morning Chili Bowl rode his bicycle to the candy store on Line Avenue to look for discarded bottles. He packed the bottles neatly in the wire basket on the front of his bicycle. As he crossed the intersection of Line and Seventy-Third, a car slammed into him and just kept on going. Everyone there said that it never even slowed. The squeal of tires and the sound of the impact was heard for blocks. When I heard the neighbors yelling, I ran to see what happened. There was my best friend lying in the street with broken glass all over him and blood flowing from his head.

I looked at the crowd around us and asked, "What happened?"

Someone said angrily, "A white lady hit Chili Bowl and just kept on going."

I knelt next to his body and opened his eyes with my fingers. "Chili Bowl, can you hear me? Get up. Get up."

He didn't answer. He just died.

My heart felt so heavy. Warm tears streamed down my face. Just when I had found a friend, someone killed him. My anger was made bigger by the fact that the woman who hit him didn't have the decency to stop. She left him in the middle of the street to die like a dog. I ran home as fast as I could. "Mama, she killed Chili Bowl. She killed Chili Bowl. A white lady killed him. She hit him with her car. I don't have a friend no more."

Mama placed her arms around me and said, "It'll be okay. Sometimes things happen for the better, and work for the good of those that know the Lord."

Tears ran down my face. "I know the Lord didn't work *me* no good."

"You'll understand it better by and by," my mother said calmly.

"By when, Mama?"

She had no answer.

Life turned gray. I didn't go fishing anymore. School became a horrible place again. Every day brought a new version of Chili Bowl's death. As a joke, some kids lay on the ground and pretended to be dead, saying, "This is how Chili Bowl looked."

I had no one at all to talk to, to laugh with, or to play with at school. The children got meaner and started picking on me again. My savior was gone. Chili Bowl could no longer protect me as he had in the past. The teasing and insults increased. The loneliness grew unbearable.

I knew what God was trying to tell me.

You are alone.

CHAPTER **SEVEN**

I became fascinated with stealing at the age of eight. I don't know if the thrill was being able to get away with a crime, or that the crime was against the white man. Either way, it was the start of a prosperous career. I used to confiscate—read steal—cartons of cookies from the factory in town that made them, and sell them to the smaller markets in the community. I stashed them in the bushes and came back at night for them. I loaded them in my little red wagon and casually strolled down Main Street. It amazed me no one ever questioned how I got those cookies.

Negroes often got arrested for hunting animals for food. The police said it was stealing. They called it "hunting out of season." Since hunger had no season, it meant those animals had more value than we did. One summer day, I went hunting with my .22 rifle. It went fine. I killed three wild ducks and three squirrels. My family would have meat to eat that night, and some left over for the next day. I trussed the dead animals with fishing line and attached them with fishhooks to a stick I rested on my shoulder. I walked home through the woods with the bodies dangling behind me, blood soaking the back of my shirt. I was happy and fulfilled. I had done my job as a man and provider.

Almost as soon as I stepped onto Main Street, the sheriff's car pulled up alongside me. I hadn't had a run-in with the sheriff before, so I continued to walk. I had done nothing wrong. He pulled the car directly in front of me and jumped out.

"Where you goin' with those animals, boy? You steal 'em from somebody?"

I answered quickly, "No, sir. I killed them in the woods today. My family needs the meat."

He raised an eyebrow and stared me down. "My family needs meat, too, but I'm gon' have to arrest you for shooting animals out of season. It's against the law, boy. I'm gon' put your black ass in jail."

He took the meat and told me to turn around with my hands behind my back so he could handcuff me. As I did, out of nowhere, a hard object crashed against the back of my head. I fell with the world spinning around me. The sheriff had hit me with his flashlight. He kneeled next to me, flicked open the cylinder of his gun, and showed me the bullets inside.

"I've got six bullets, nigger, and I'm gon' shoot you one for every animal you killed. You got thirty seconds to get your black ass outta here or I'm gon' shoot you dead, boy."

I got up with the world a blur and ran as fast as I could. By the time I got home, I was so dizzy and exhausted I lay down in the shade under the tree and passed out, lying on my stomach.

Sometime later, I heard Mama screaming, "They killed my baby. They killed my baby. Those bastards! I'm gon' get my shotgun and kill them, too."

I opened my eyes. "What's wrong, Mama? Are you okay? Did something happen to my sisters?"

Mama dropped to my side, shaking, she was so relieved. "I thought you were dead, Richard."

"Why?"

"'Cause you got blood all over the back of your shirt."

I told my mom about going hunting and the blood on my shirt, but before I could tell her the rest, she yelped excitedly, "Thank God, we got meat today. We can eat like kings. I'm gon' do some real good cookin' on that meat, Sonny."

I lowered my eyes. "Mama, the sheriff took all of the meat and hit me upside my head with his flashlight. He threatened to shoot me six times, so I ran."

I saw a look on my mama's face I had never seen, a sadness that seemed too deep to measure. "Richard, I love you and your sisters more than anything in this world, but if I had known life would be like this for you children, I'm not sure I would've had none of y'all."

I could see the hurt, not just in her eyes, but in her walk. She climbed the steps slowly, head hung low. She had a defeated spirit and a depleted heart. On the last step, she looked back and said, "I thought you was dead. I'm glad you alive, Richard."

So was I.

The beating set me back a bit but I recovered. The sheriff might have taken my kill, but not my ambition—my desire to steal. That grew as fast as I saw opportunities. At twelve, I started a produce garden in our backyard to stock a farm stand. Whatever I could not grow, I confiscated—stole—from white people. I stole watermelons, peaches, strawberries, blackberries, tomatoes, hickory nuts, and pecans. Pecans were my biggest seller during Christmas. When I was at school, I hired the men who loitered on street corners to work the farm stand for me.

I earned twenty-four dollars a week. Determined to make more, I confiscated cotton at night while the field hands and supervisors slept. Confident, I confiscated cotton five to six times a year. Occasionally, I killed someone's cow, goat, or pig and sold the meat from a wagon I pulled around the neighborhood. By the time I was thirteen, my business ventures were profitable enough to move us into a little-better house at 514 East Seventy-Seventh. We put down half the cost of the land up front and agreed to pay the balance six months later. School took a backseat because I was too busy trying to make money. Still, I refused to neglect my education. I read books and tried to be a good student, but a new conflict emerged. I fancied myself a fine horn and harmonica player. I also played a mean set of drums. I wanted to be in the school band, but Mr. H, the band director, considered me a troublemaker and refused to let me play.

Mr. H was a high yellow Negro who thought his light skin made him better than those of us who were dark-complexioned. He didn't see that it didn't matter a damn to white folks. To them, he was still just another nigger.

"I heard around town you a big thief," he told me. "That's a easy way to get killed. I got some good children in my band and I ain't gon' let you come around and poison they minds. Boy, you the devil. You go round stealin' from them white folks. Them people ain't done nothin' to you. Why you steal their stuff?"

I shrugged. I didn't explain my motives. He wouldn't understand them. I was supposed to accept his word as law, but I couldn't. I found the solution to my problem in my new best friend, a boy named Lil Man, who ran with the Cedar Grove Gang. Lil Man always had a sly look on his face and wasn't afraid of anyone or anything. He also had a reputation for stealing in broad daylight, so I dared him to steal the decoration horn off the top of the iceman's truck so I could play it in the band.

"I'll give you twenty-five cents if you can get it," I promised.

Never one to walk away from a challenge, Lil Man gave an airy wave. "Man, I can steal anything. One time I crawled under Old Man Thomas's fence and stole a pig. And I'm gon' do it agin, Richard."

Old Man Thomas was a white farmer who lived on the outskirts of town. A member of the Ku Klux Klan, Thomas had already killed two Negroes who tried to imitate Lil Man's success.

Lil Man boasted, "I crawled under the fence and grabbed one of those slimy pigs. It kept squealing so I hit him on the head with a big rock. Was my mama happy when I got home? She cleaned that pig up and cooked it. We sure 'nuff had some good eatin'."

Sure enough, the next morning when I went to the well to get some water, Lil Man was waiting for me on the back porch with my new horn.

"You got my money, Richard?" he asked with a grin.

I dug deep into my pocket, pulled out twenty-five cents, and gave it to him.

Lil Man smiled easy-like. "Let me know if you need me to steal somethin' else. I'll steal it for another quarter."

At that moment, I admired everything about him. "I don't need nothin' else," I said. "But thanks a lot."

Lil Man turned his cap backward, grinned, and walked away.

That was the last time I saw him. Three days later, some boys hunting in the woods found his lifeless body hanging from a tree. Both his hands had been cut off. Rumor had it that Mr. Thomas was having a Ku Klux Klan meeting when Lil Man tried to steal another of his pigs. The Klan caught Lil Man and decided to make an example out of him. They bound his hands and feet and tied a handkerchief around his mouth. They cut off both his hands with an ax and lynched his shocked body from a tree. Then they hung Lil Man's hands on the fence as a warning to other niggers who thought about stealing.

There was no formal investigation. No one was ever questioned. Nobody was able to prove who killed Lil Man because no one ever tried.

For a long time, guilt prevented me from using the horn. Anger won out. Lil Man wasn't going to die for nothing. If Mr. H wouldn't let me play with the band officially, I would play with it unofficially. The horn was too old and battered to play, but inside was a small opening into which I inserted a whistle. I stuffed old rags around it to keep it from falling out. It had the strangest sound I'd ever heard. It sounded like a hurt chirping bird and a crying baby. Whenever the band played, I hid out of sight and blew my man-made horn.

Like a screaming banshee, I blew it and blew it. Every time I blew it, I thought about Lil Man. That sound was *his* sound. That cry was his last on earth. Sometimes, anger overrides fear. I had enough anger at that moment that if I'd had a good gun I might've killed somebody. Instead, I decided to complete what Lil Man had started. Not only would I steal the white man's pigs, I'd take an ax and kill them. I would steal their cows, their horses, their wagons, their mules. I would steal anything that wasn't nailed down—and if it *was* nailed down, I'd find a way to un-nail it and take it, too.

It was my own personal revolution.

First, I made Old Man Thomas pay for killing Lil Man over a goddamned slimy dirty-ass pig. He had a beautiful black stallion, a prized possession. He loved that horse more than he loved his kids. He used to take it to horse shows, and it always won first place. For days, I snuck into the woods and hid behind a tree and watched him pamper the horse. He kept it in a fenced corral and brushed its coat gently and talked to it like it was human. One night, I went to the corral, let the stallion out, and quietly led it away. I sold it for fifty dollars to a man who said Thomas owed him some money. I would have shot it, but I got more pleasure knowing it was still alive and Thomas couldn't get it back.

I stole what he loved most, but that was just another lesson. We were a long way from being even.

CHAPTER **EIGHT**

Reputation is everything in a small town where everybody knows everybody else's business. I was a teen now, with some money in my pocket, big and strong, looking for respect. I was the first guy to start a fight and the last one to back down from one. Lil Man's death made something go cold within me. I grew from a heated boy into an angry young man, filled with rage. When I couldn't get the white man's respect, I dishonored him by stealing from him. I had no sense of guilt or remorse. I was the injured party. I "confiscated" because it made me feel powerful and in control. My stealing mocked whites because they weren't able to stop me. What they took from me was theirs. What I took back was mine.

It seemed to me that Louisiana was the most violent place in the world. The older I got, the worse it grew. People went to church and cried out to the Lord to stop the suffering, but it seemed like the devil was loose on earth. Hatred consumed me. I was in a barren land, unproductive, unprofitable, worthless. I could not escape it. Racism was suffocating my soul. Every day was exhausting, not knowing who I was, where I could go, when I could speak.

Adding fuel to the ever-burning fire was the Ku Klux Klan, a terrorist organization of nightriders in flowing white gowns and hoods. They used God to justify hatred, wrapping themselves in Christianity and stealing its holiest symbol, the cross. Cross burning was a sacred Klan rite, inviting God to fill a world of darkness with His white light. Hiding behind a twisted patriotism, they wanted America to be a white man's country, exclusively. Their efforts to ensure that were violent, destructive, and pitiless.

The Klan rampaged through the South, confident it could violate us with impunity. They got away with murder, protected by a secret conspiracy of police, judges, and jurors. Those sworn to protect and serve became the killers of a generation, or silent witnesses to it. They trapped my friends and family in a reign of inhuman terror, lynchings, floggings, castrations, murders, fires, and relentless intimidation.

In the 1950s, punishment for a black man "getting out of place" was swift and brutal. Crowds of southern whites armed with sticks, bottles, knives, and guns surrounded their victims and eagerly inflicted pain or death. In the summer of 1964, three civil rights workers were murdered and their bodies found buried beneath a dam. That was rare. The Klan usually buried its victims so deep the bodies couldn't be resurrected even on Judgment Day.

Only one time did they ever come close to getting to me. To this day, I don't really remember the reason for the fight, or why it escalated to the point where I was fighting off three white men in the street, covered in dirt and blood, while a crowd watched. I looked up, and there was my father standing among the white crowd, watching me get beaten without so much as lifting a finger to help me. He didn't call out. He didn't wade in. He just watched as I tried to survive the onslaught, and as the mob turned in his direction seeking another black man to target with their anger and hatred, he ran off, leaving me there alone.

It is a terrible thing to be so unloved, to know your father would rather let you die than lift a finger to help you, to watch him run off and leave you all alone. I knew he didn't love me. I knew he was worthless. I knew he was the bane of my existence when he made all those babies in my mother and treated her so badly. But this kind of pain, I had never known. This was no refusal to give me a quarter to go to the movies. It was no casual passing without even a hello. It was a rejection so cold it remains burnt in my memory and, in the end, did what even white people could never do, hurt me so deep in my soul that I have never forgotten or forgiven.

Every time I broke the rules, it brought me closer to death, but it never stopped me. Anger was my life. I found strength challenging the Klan to see how far I could go. The WHITES ONLY and COLORED ONLY signs on water fountains and buildings and restaurant counters were my flags, symbols of my fight. I was playing with fire and I got to like it. I entered stores through the front door. I put money in clerks' hands. I walked tall and proud. I browsed around. I picked up a pack of Kool-Aid and went right to the counter to pay for it.

The owner scowled, "Boy, the back door is for coloreds. Now get out of here and come back in through the back door."

I stood my ground.

Thump! A bat crashed against my head. I fell to my knees and fell forward with warm blood flowing down my forehead and into my eyes.

The owner yelled, "Throw that nigger in the street before he bleeds all over my store."

White men grabbed my feet and dragged me out. My head bounced down the front steps. The pain was excruciating. Blood was everywhere. No one called a doctor. I lay in the street moaning. Didn't they see me?

"Will somebody help me?" I gasped.

No one helped. No one cared. Finally, the police arrived, and without question or hesitation, cuffed me and threw me into the back of the police car. My crime was wanting to be treated like a man. If I was a criminal for that, things were going to get a lot worse very soon.

My stealing increased. The more I stole the more I invalidated the strength of the white people who wanted to keep me down. But I had to be real careful. If I was caught in the act, I would be tortured and killed just like Lil Man, and my hands hung from a fence. That said, it was easy to spot danger in the form of white people. None of them would have any problem turning me in. The greater problem was other blacks. We were all encouraged to be "good" niggers and rewarded for turning in other blacks. Whites taught Negroes the more they ratted out the "bad" Negroes, the better off the "good ones" would be. They were given gifts—a hog, a pig, or a chicken—in exchange for exposing another man's activities. To me, a black man who would turn in another black man was almost worse than any white. It made me sick.

As my war grew deadlier, one of these casualties was an old black man named Mr. Percy. No one knew if Percy was his first name or last, everybody just called him that. He was a tall, heavyset man about fifty years old. According to Mr. Percy, his left arm had been severed at the elbow years before by five white men in a pickup who jumped him coming home from the fish creek. They punched him in the stomach and pushed him on the ground. Four of them held his hands and legs. The fifth man took a blade and sawed his arm off at the elbow.

He told the story like it was just a matter of fact, strangely without anger or resentment. Nor did he say one derogatory word about the men who harmed him. I cried uncontrollably, lost in pity and sorrow for him.

"Why did they cut your arm off, Mr. Percy?"

"Them old hunters wouldn't feed their dogs for ten, eleven, or twelve days. Then they would run 'em and work 'em real hard. By then, they'd be starving. So the white men made a game out of finding Negroes and cutting off parts of their bodies and feeding them to the dogs."

It took me a long time to sleep, digesting that.

At the height of my war against white people, stealing and selling everything I could take, Mr. Percy told me, "Richard, if you don't stop stealing cookies and taking the white man's cotton, both your arms and legs gon' get cut off. Then you won't have no hands to steal with and no legs to run with. If them people knew how much you stole from them, they just as soon kill your mama and your sisters, too."

Maybe he was talking out of concern. To me, it felt like he was siding with my enemies. Three weeks later, Mr. Percy stopped me near a farm owned by a white man named Stabler, as I was on my way to steal his cotton.

"You out there stealin' again, Richard? Ain't no need to lie, son. I know you stealin' Mr. Stabler's cotton 'cause I seen ya out there one night with my own eyes. I'm a night watchman over at his cotton gin. Richard, if you keep it up, I'm gon' have to turn you in."

I put my face close to his. "I don't plan to stop takin' nothin' from the white bastards. All they do is take from us. They take our lives, they rape our women, they drown us in the lake and drag us through the street till we dead. They embarrass our parents by calling them aunt and uncle. They been treatin' us like this from one generation to the next, my parents, their parents, their parents' parents. You such a loyal nigger, you work hard for them white bastards all night and still have to push your ice cream cart by day to make more money 'cause they ain't paying you a damn thing." I was hot, and crazy with rage. "Mr. Percy, if you ever tell the white devil on me or tell anybody else, I'll take an ax and cut off your other arm and both your legs."

I pulled the ice pick I kept with me all the time out of my jacket. I used it a lot when I confiscated things. I put it against Mr. Percy's throat. "Now, you listen up. I'll be stealin' from Mr. Stabler's place every night from now on. You *my* night watchman now and if you see the white man gettin' close, you betta let me know 'cause if you don't, I'll kill you and your whole family."

Mr. Percy was wild-eyed. He said, trembling, "You cut Jamie Lee's throat, didn't ya?"

"Yes, I cut his throat," I bragged.

Jamie Lee Amos lived in Cedar Grove on Fairfield and Seventy-Third Street. I got in a fight with him at Carver High School at a basketball game, and Jamie Lee's gang vowed to get me. When he and his friends surrounded me, I grabbed the person closest to me, who happened to be Jamie Lee, and stuck the pick in his throat. He didn't die, but he sure bled a lot, and everybody got the message not to mess with me one more time.

I held that same ice pick at Mr. Percy's throat till he swore he would never tell the white man what I was doing. I was angry with Mr. Percy because he personified the typical Negro.

Maybe I saw some of myself in him and I couldn't bear it. It killed me he was so goddamn eager to turn me in.

I continued my acts of defiance against white people, while other disturbing events were taking place all around me. Shreveport hadn't built any swimming pools in our neighborhood, so the only decent place to swim was at Lakeside, next to Booker T. Washington High School. Gang members controlled this area and beat up black kids who walked past their corners. Shreveport had more than its share of gangs. There were the Line Street Boys, the Cedar Grove Gang, the .22 Caliber Gang, the Crooks, and the Hustlers. As with society's current plague of gangbangers, it surprised and disgusted me how easily blacks could terrorize their own. Decades later, my struggle in Compton acquainted me with gangs of the same mentality, who destroyed black communities by preying on other blacks without mercy.

With gang violence running high, black parents warned their children to stay away from Lakeside. My mom said, "Richard, promise me you won't go swimming out there. A lotta strange things goin' on at them places. Maybe you oughta just swim in the ditches like the other children."

All the homes in Cedar Grove had drainage ditches around them. During the rainy season, they kept water from flooding the houses. Even more practical, you could jump over the ditches into the fields when whites chased us in their trucks, and they couldn't cross over to catch you. They were also an ideal place to swim. However, as a teenager I had long outgrown swimming in ditches. That was child's play.

Several mysterious drownings of Negro children occurred that summer. We believed whites were drowning them if they got caught swimming by themselves at the popular swimming holes. Rumor held that the murderers bragged around town about how they "drowned that black-ass nigger." In spite of

the danger, some Negro boys insisted on swimming there. I
was one of them. We swam in the Ollie Fountain and the Red
River. It was a case of sink or swim, since most of us were inex-
perienced swimmers.

At the time, my best friend was Augustine Gardner. I thought
no one would ever replace Chili Bowl or Lil Man, but as the
years went on, Augustine did. We were inseparable. We shared
common interests like shooting marbles, fishing, hunting, and
swimming. I loved having a best friend, someone to talk to about
my plans and dreams. I wanted to protect him, as Chili Bowl
had once protected me, so even though we were best friends I
never let him in on my business schemes that involved confisca-
tion. If I ever got caught, Augustine wouldn't be an accomplice
to my crimes.

Like my father, Augustine's father had walked away from
his family and Augustine had to take over the man-of-the-
house role, too. We worked hard to help our families. We
made a pact that one day we would leave Shreveport together
and see what the rest of the world was like.

It never happened. Augustine went swimming alone in the
Red River. Some of our buddies found him floating facedown
in the water. Someone had bound his feet and hands and he
was naked. Rumors spread through the neighborhood. Some
claimed Augustine's genitals had been chopped off. Others
said his body was tarred and feathered. Yet another said the
fish had eaten his eyes out. To me, it didn't matter how he
died. I could not dismiss the terrible fact that Augustine Gardner was dead at sixteen. For the third time in my young life, I
had lost my best friend.

From that day on, I made myself a promise never to take a
chance on friendship again.

To this day, I have kept that promise.

CHAPTER **NINE**

To the amazement of most of the people who knew me, it was 1959 and I was still alive. Wrongful deaths, accidental drownings, and false imprisonments had taken their toll on the community, and few understood why I hadn't suffered the same fate. Shreveport was a mortuary, death was its business, and those who remained were dying. We were detoured into back roads, sidelines, ditches, and alleyways. Tired of being a silent passenger on the road of life, I wanted control of my fate.

Despite the plight of my people, or perhaps because of it, in my heart I grew married to the idea of achieving the American dream. I was a businessman and I was a thief. In short, I was a capitalist. I felt that too many of my people looked to the white man or his government to provide for them. If my fate was really in my hands, and I wanted to rise above poverty, I began to think I had to leave Shreveport.

My family reacted to my idea of leaving Shreveport with dire skepticism. I understood their reluctance. My mom had gotten work as a janitor at the Little Hope School and no matter how little hope it held, she wanted me to have the same job. I couldn't bear to think of a life like that. As her criticism increased, my desire to escape grew. Needing a listening ear and an understanding heart, I turned to the one person I knew who could advise me—an eighty-year-old foot soldier in the army of the Lord named Mr. Beaumont.

Mr. Beaumont was the preacher at the Church of God in Christ on East Eightieth Street and Fairfield, a church he had built when he was seventy years old. Mr. Beaumont collected the food that supermarkets threw out at the end of every day, fruit, bread, meat, and canned goods. He loaded it all on a wagon and pulled it through the street, ringing a bell as he came through, so people would know he was there and come out to get some food. For many, he was a godsend.

Mr. Beaumont went about his work in his own quiet but forceful way. He provided for many who could not provide for themselves. He was neither subservient nor arrogant, and when he spoke, his words went straight to my heart.

"God don't need no coward soldier, Richard," was his bold command I liked best.

Everyone credited Mr. Beaumont's longevity to his unyielding faith. Trusting, never doubting, he believed one day God would wash all the tears away. He had no words of revenge or retaliation. He spent his time reading the Bible and took every passage to heart. His message to the congregation was to rejoice and give thanks to God and to "love thine enemy."

Love thine enemy? I wanted to kill the enemy. It was inconceivable to me that Mr. Beaumont could rejoice in the midst of pain and find peace in the middle of a racial war. Yet, I respected him deeply. Perhaps it was just that Mr. Beaumont stood so steadfastly for something, something definite, something real. He had substance, unlike my father, who stood for nothing and went where the wind blew. Despite my own notion of what was right and wrong, Mr. Beaumont was as solid as a deep-rooted tree, a man of conviction.

I followed the railroad tracks that divided the Negro community from the white, to Mr. Beaumont's house on the outskirts of town. The farther I got, the more uninviting it became. The poorest of the poor lived here, in houses varying from tiny cottages to dilapidated shacks with cardboard windows.

Mr. Beaumont lived in a small wooden house with no running water and no inside plumbing. Surprisingly, he had a TV. Across the road, a cotton field stretched across the horizon with pickers moving slowly across it while Mr. Beaumont drove a mule-drawn plow wagon.

When he saw me on the porch, he called, "Be right there, son. Have a seat."

I wasn't sure how to begin. I wanted to talk about so many things. Thoughts cascaded through my head as Mr. Beaumont drove over and shook the reins off the mules. He mounted the porch steps, mopping his brow, and said kindly, "Now, Richard, what's all this about? Why you come see me?"

Looking at his wrinkled face, gray hair, and honest eyes, I thought Mr. Beaumont was the model of the southern Negro. He was dressed in overalls, work boots, and a straw sun hat. He moved slowly and made no move to prompt me, and words suddenly poured from my mouth.

"Mr. Beaumont, I been searching for my piece of the American pie. You think they give some of that pie to Negroes? Even if they don't, I want mine. If I have to die to get it, that's okay. Ain't gon' let nothing or nobody steal my hope, 'cause I been dreaming too long. It's got to be better somewhere, and I'm gon' find out where. You know what I mean, Mr. Beaumont?"

He wiped an old kerchief over his face and nodded slowly. "Only trouble is, in order to find the pie you lookin' for, you might have to leave *this* place, 'cause you ain't gon' find it here in Louisiana. Texas, either."

Was this the affirmation I had come for? "So I should leave?"

"Son, I've been alive 'bout eighty years now and done lived long enough to know, you might have to go to another *country* to do the things you talkin' 'bout." He laughed. "Them white folks ain't gon' give you no pie. Crust, either," he said jokingly.

He gestured around. "All I have is a truck, two mules, a church house, and this old three-bedroom shack that's falling apart. Everything else, Richard, they took. But I still got something. I got Jesus. Here now, come with me."

He motioned me to follow him to the wagon and his hands trembled as he slowly pulled himself into the driver's seat. The two mules hitched to the wagon were as black as night. I noticed that one had a short leg as I climbed aboard, but the ride was still a smooth one. We traveled in silence down the dusty road and the quiet settled in all around us as the light faded and the first night insects began to murmur. We passed shack after shack and finally came to a large piece of land that stretched as far as the eye could see.

"I used to own this land a long time ago," Mr. Beaumont said. "Me, my wife, and children lived here for many years. We had people workin' for us pickin' cotton back then. A poor white family, the Dixons, lived just down the road. It was so hard back then, sometimes we gave them food 'cause they didn't have nothing. We was good neighbors and got along pretty good, but after a while Mr. Dixon started acting a little funny. The chillin used to play together but he stopped 'em. I couldn't figure it out at first, but I started seeing a lot of strange white men going to his house.

"Sometimes, they'd walk down here and stand in the road lookin' at me plowing the field with my mule. I heard them men gave Dixon a hard time 'bout a nigger having a mule and he didn't have one. Seemed like he got meaner and meaner and he ended up treatin' me just like the rest of the white folks. He started calling me nigger, too.

"We never had a lot of trouble in this part of town with white folks come to burn you out and things. One night, we heard a lot of noise outside and I got my rifle and went to see what the racket was about. There was a cross burning in the front yard. Didn't need nobody to tell me where it came from—it was the Klan. People in the neighborhood got worried 'cause they thought the Klan was gon' start botherin' us, but it seemed like it was just me they was after. They'd ride by in a truck hollering and calling me nigger.

"One day, Dixon and two white men caught me by surprise while I was plowing the field. One of 'em was a tall ugly man with eyes like the devil himself. He kept staring at me and I could feel the hate. He said, 'How a poor nigger like you get enough money to buy that mule? Dixon here is a white man and he don't have a mule.'

"I just said, 'Yes, sir.'

"He said, 'You think you an important nigger, don't you, boy?'

"I said, 'No, sir,' and kept my head down 'cause if I looked him in the eye he'd a thought I was disrespectin' him.

"He said, 'A lotta things can happen to a smart-ass nigger like you. You better watch yourself, boy.'

"I said, 'Yes, sir.'

"When I got up the next morning, my mule was laying in the field dead. Somebody cut his throat and he bled to death. Wasn't no need to call the police 'cause the law wasn't on a Negro side, no way."

I nodded vigorously. "That's why I wanna leave this place and go north, Mr. Beaumont. Betcha they don't treat Negroes like dogs there."

He just nodded kind of wearylike and didn't say anything, just flicked the reins.

"Mr. Beaumont, did you ever want to fight them back?" I asked.

His tired old smile seemed to come from a long way off. "I wanted to fight back plenty of times, but I didn't. Wasn't 'cause I was no coward, either. Just I wasn't a man no more. Them white folks took my manhood away from me every time they beat me, every time they called me nigger, every time they called me boy. They took my manhood every time the whip hit my back, every time my head got kicked in by a boot. They took it every time the boss man asked me, 'Are you a nigger or a Negro?' And he'd kick me in my stomach till I screamed, 'I'm a nigger, boss. I'm a nigger. Please don't kick me no mo' . . .'" Tears flowed from his eyes. He shook his fist. "But I *am* a man, Richard. I got up. It takes a strong man to be beat down and keep getting up."

He pointed toward the land, colored gray by the evening mist. "One night, they came out here dressed in them white masks and robes. They set my barn on fire and my animals just burnt up. My wife knew something was wrong that night 'fore it happened. She say God showed her a vision in her dream. When the dogs started barking, my wife and the children went out the back door and hid in the woods. We had a shed built out there behind some bushes and the only way you seen it, you had to know it was there. No sooner had they got out the back door, men broke the front door down. They beat me, broke my ribs, and knocked my teeth out. One of 'em said, 'Ain't no nigger got no business owning no land. Now sign this paper or we gon' burn your house to the ground.' I signed it and lost my land. One of them said, 'Now pay the nigger what the land's worth.' Another man dropped a nickel on the floor, and they left."

Mr. Beaumont stared off into his own personal hell, a place I would not fully understand until years later. He shrugged. "I used to be so angry 'bout that, but none of us don't own nothin'. Everything I got belong to God, even my life. They can't take that 'less God give it to 'em. I'm too old to fight a war I can't win, too old. All this will be over soon and I'll finally have some peace."

He looked at me. In the twilight, his face was hard set, his eyes steely, so different from the preacher I had always known.

"Richard, the only way you gon' get some peace on this earth is to get right with God and make sure you leave Shreveport. You say you want a piece of the American pie. America ain't gave us nothin' but hell, so don't think they gon' give you a piece of anything. If you get a piece, it'll be spoiled, or rotten."

He flicked the reins hard. The mules surged. There was wind now. It stirred the tops of the trees like a storm was coming. He turned his gaze on me and it was a fearful thing.

"Richard, in my heart, I know God's got something special for you to do, but you can't get it done here. Get out of here while you can. God'll make a way. Ain't nothing here for you, son, nothing at all."

CHAPTER TEN

My mother's brother, Uncle Roman Metcalf, lived in Chicago. He worked as a construction supervisor. Always the big shot, Uncle Roman visited Shreveport every summer, gracing our neighborhood like royalty. He was tall, muscular, and good-looking, and his flamboyant, loud-colored suits, spit-shined shoes, and wide-brimmed hats mesmerized the local women. Young and old, they swooned over him like he was king.

Roman's sleek talk and hip walk made a major impression on me at seventeen. He was the epitome of flash and style, cruising through town in his fancy car, puffing on a cigar, his diamond-ringed hand resting elegantly on the wheel. Roman's stories about Chicago thrilled me. He gave life to a place I'd only heard about. He filled my mind with thoughts of skyscrapers as tall as the eye could see, rows of beautiful picket-fenced houses on wide clean streets, and busy family-owned stores where the owners knew you by name and put your bill on a tab. His Chicago was not a backward jungle filled with white hoods, nor an inferno that burned our homes and engulfed our hearts. No slave consciousness ruled it, and segregation had no venue. It was a place of hope, togetherness, and love.

My talk with Mr. Beaumont lay heavily on my mind. When I added his words to the vision my uncle created, my direction seemed obvious. I would leave Shreveport and make a new start in Chicago with Uncle Roman.

Four months after my eighteenth birthday, in the spring of 1960, when my sisters were asleep, I talked to my mother about leaving home.

"Mama, what would you think if I moved to Chicago?"

Excited, I told her all the wonderful things Uncle Roman told me. Mama looked at me narrowly. "I knew you had something on your mind. Richard, you been acting strange lately. You keep disrespectin' those white folks and they goin' to kill you."

"But . . ."

"But nothin'. Me and your sisters can get killed 'cause of you. Those crazy people can set our house on fire while we're sleeping and shoot us if we try to run out. Shreveport is your home and there ain't no other place you can go to. Chicago won't be no different. No matter what you heard 'bout it, you gon' be just another nigger no matter where you go. The sooner you understand this, the better off you'll be, the better you'll live."

I was silent. Was she right?

She kept it up. "I don't know why you feel this way or what's happening to you, but there's so many things you can do right here in Shreveport and be happy. I got a good job as a janitor at Little Hope now and we not doin' so bad. Why you don't see that, Richard?"

I was having trouble seeing anything. It was so cold outside that our fireplace was no competition for the freezing temperature. Stacks of wood lay waiting to be tossed into the fire. I felt my resolve weaken—and for all I know, I might still be in Shreveport, except for the sudden harsh white light that filled the windows and the loud angry voices all around the house. With a big *thump*, the front door crashed in and policemen flooded the room.

Mama screamed. "What's the matter? What y'all want here?"

One shined the flashlight in her face. "Is that your boy?"

Mama shoved me aside. "What y'all want with him?"

One of the officers pinned me with his stare. "Somebody said they saw him throw a rock through the A&P window."

By now, my sisters were awake and crying, afraid the white folks were going to burn our house down. "They gon' hurt us?" Faye asked.

I said, "No, we gon' be okay. Be quiet."

The police grabbed me and put handcuffs on my wrists. I was confused and scared. Mama rushed to my sisters and hugged them.

"Stop crying, y'all. Richard gon' be all right 'cause he ain't done nothing wrong."

They tossed me into the backseat of the police car, barefoot, half dressed, and took me to jail. One busted me with his nightstick. I was detained in a cell with no phone call, no bail, no right to counsel. Mama didn't know anything about the law, but she knew I needed help right away. She sent for my uncle Roman. He came to the police station dressed to the nines, throwing around legal terms and fancy phrases left and right. He told them I was only fifteen years old and couldn't be held as an adult and, to my complete shock, convinced those bastards to release me.

I had been beat up and scared. It made my determination to leave stronger than ever. I told Uncle Roman I wanted to go to Chicago with him.

"Richard," he said, "seeing how the police felt about you, I think you should make plans to get out of town sooner rather than later."

I agreed with Uncle Roman. I made plans. For the next few months, I was a model of humility and servitude. I camouflaged my hatred with a grin and a lowered head. But revenge was my ultimate goal. Before I left, I planned to give back a piece of what had been given to me all my life. I was going to infiltrate the Ku Klux Klan. I wanted to wear the mask of hatred and racism. I wanted to hold life and death in my hands. Power was just a white sheet and hood away.

My plan had to be perfect, because one mistake would mean my death. The mere thought of what I planned energized and overwhelmed me at the same time. Getting the traditional Klan attire was easy. My friends Big Mo and Louis, members of the Cedar Grove Gang, were having sex with a white farmer's daughter named Lucy Clavens. Lucy did anything for sex. Her mother died when she was five years old and her father, Billy, raised her. Soon, Lucy replaced her mother in every way. Two children were born from this incest, a secret everyone in town knew, but ignored. The same kind of secret was that her father was Klan.

Lucy was like an obedient puppy, and I knew she would tell Louis where her father kept his Klan outfit. Big Mo found it just where she said it was, hanging on a nail in the toolshed. My concern was hiding my skin color. The mask only had little round eyeholes so it showed no skin, and the gown was floor-length. I had my sisters buy makeup from the pharmacy and we experimented with it playfully when Mama was working. My sisters had no idea it was anything but play as we tested combinations of color until we had one that turned my hands into convincing white skin at night.

After dark, I rode my dark blue bicycle into a white neighborhood with the KKK outfit neatly folded inside my jacket. I hid the bicycle in the bushes, walked three blocks, ducked into an alley, and put on the hood and robe and rubbed my hands in the makeup. It was a moonless night and the trees barely moved. Even the insect sounds were soft. I walked two blocks before selecting my victims—a white farmer and his teenaged son sitting on a park bench, smoking and drinking. They both wore work boots, T-shirts, and overalls. I smelled their smoke, heard the scratchy sound as they rubbed their stubbly faces.

My hatred was up, and so was my longing to pay back somebody, anybody, for everything that ever happened to me. I felt the power anonymity gave me. I picked up a stick. My attack was quick and vicious. I crept up behind them in the darkness, brought the stick down on their heads, and they cried out and fell to the ground.

I ran away as fast as I could, taking deep breaths and whispering to myself, "Relax, stay cool." I pulled off the outfit, slipped it inside my jacket, rubbed off the makeup, and ran back to my bike. I pedaled slowly down the street until I was outside the white neighborhood, then pedaled like the devil himself was chasing me. When I pulled into my yard, my heart was racing from the adrenaline rush.

That's when I knew.

I was going to do it again.

The event was totally intoxicating. Capture meant death for me and my family, but I was willing to take that risk. The next day, word spread about the attack at the hands of the Klan. The son swore he saw the Klansman as he ran away into the night. Here was an unexpected twist. I had stirred up controversy and made whites their own enemies.

Two weeks later, I strolled into Broadmoor, a neighborhood nestled between two hills. I had parked my bicycle a quarter of a mile away and was wearing the KKK robe, looking for my next victim. Suddenly, a car drove toward me with its lights on. It was a police car. It was too late to duck into the bushes. The red and blue lights on top of the police car flashed.

Panic-stricken, I froze.

One of the cops rolled down his window. I smelled cigarette smoke. "Looks like somebody's going coon hunting tonight, eh? The boys are all around the corner." He sounded happy, just out for a night of fun. He tossed the cigarette butt into the road and waved at me, then rolled up the window as the car sped away.

I stood there openmouthed. It was the acid test. It was incredible. The police thought I was Klan.

I walked around the corner. In the headlights of a pickup truck, I saw three Klansmen in uniform. One was holding a rifle. The other two were in the truck bed, struggling to hold down a Negro boy who was fighting for his life to get free. I didn't know what to do. To be honest, at first I didn't think about the boy, who was likely to be murdered that night. I am sorry to say, at that moment, I was only concerned about myself.

Before I could do anything, the driver called out to me in a hoarse voice, "Hey, we got that lazy nigger that ran away from Melvin's place. We're gonna take him in the woods and shoot him dead. Get in."

I climbed in the back and it seemed like an eternity as we

sped through the woods, bumping up and down on the deeply furrowed dirt road. Headlights bounced over bushes and trees. Spooky shadows slid by. I was ready to run or kill if they discovered me. I tried to calm my breathing. I wondered if they could smell my fear. Would I make it out alive?

We stopped in a clearing and the truck shuddered to a stop, engine clicking as it cooled. The men dragged the crying boy from the back. One said, "Shut up, boy, nobody can hear you out here."

I was trying to figure out my next move when the hoarse-voiced driver handed me his rifle and grinned. "If you shoot that nigger right between the eyes, it'll burst his head wide open."

Laughter filled the air when someone else said, "Instead of the headless horseman, we'll have the headless nigger. He don't need a head no way 'cause ain't a goddamn thing in it."

Standing on the dark earth, harsh light flooding the clearing, the power was mine. I had a gun. I could get one before they even knew what was happening. Then I could kill the other. I surely had the right to kill them. I tightened my finger on the trigger. An eye for an eye, a tooth for a tooth, an enemy for a friend . . .

I pointed the barrel toward the sky and let off two rounds. They froze. I pointed the rifle at them. "Let the boy go," I ordered.

One said in surprise, "What the hell is wrong with you?"

"Let the boy go," I said again and cocked the rifle. They looked at me like I was crazy but backed away from the frightened boy.

I said, "Get outta here, boy."

At first the boy didn't move, probably afraid I would shoot him in the back.

I barked angrily, "Get your ass outta here!"

He bolted through the dark woods like a jackrabbit.

Angry voices came from behind the hoods. "How could you let that nigger get away?"

I could kill them. I could pay them back for the beatings. I could have my revenge. I had my targets. I wanted to pay them back for Chili Bowl and Augustine and Mr. Beaumont, for everyone who was ever kicked or cheated and left to carry the pain of it with them in their soul. The feeling of wanting it so bad started in my guts and crept up to my chest. It slid into my head and I felt dizzy with power and hatred. Just like them. That was the thought that stopped me. I didn't want to confront that, but there it was. Maybe it was my mother's teachings, or something deep inside me, but there it was. When it came to cold-blooded murder, I was not, in the end, just like them.

I gestured with the rifle toward the woods and said, "Start walking."

As soon as they left the clearing, I threw the rifle in the truck and drove off. I had driven the truck for the fence company many times, so I knew how. After a while, I saw the Red River. As soon as I found an opening in the trees, I drove the truck into the water with the rifle and the KKK uniform inside and walked back to town. When I got to my bicycle, I pedaled home as fast as I could. The cool night air, like a tranquilizer, calmed my nerves.

Once home, I sat on the back steps and replayed the night's events in my mind over and over again. I was furious with myself that I hadn't shot those men. I was more angry about that than happy about saving that boy. It made one thing clear. My rebellious nature and refusal to bow down made me the white man's permanent enemy. I would die if I stayed.

The thought of leaving Shreveport filled my heart with grief, because I would be leaving my mother and sisters. But Mama wouldn't come to Chicago with me. No matter how much I argued, she just couldn't see her way out of where she had lived all her life. No matter. I had to go. Anger threatening to grow out of control was brewing inside me. The same violence that instilled fear in my people had taken root in me. I was a time bomb waiting to explode, and the only way to defuse it was for me to leave.

I felt tears come to my eyes as a wave of emotional fatigue hit me. Sometimes a man gets so tired he can't stand it anymore. There comes a time when you can't take being abused anymore; a time you get so tired of people taking bats to your body and chasing you with dogs and guns, you can't take it one day more. I was tired of not being a free man. I was tired of being pushed around. I was tired of being hated. I was tired of fighting. It was too much. My body couldn't take any more. Inside every part of me was a weariness so deep that all I wanted to do was lie down and sleep and surrender to whatever God there was so that He should let me just die and be free of all this. My shoulders couldn't hold up under the weight any longer. My back was breaking.

I was worn out and worn down, and Chicago beckoned like a woman who wanted me.

I was heading for paradise.

CHAPTER **ELEVEN**

Six months after the police arrested me in my house and Uncle Roman came to my rescue, I lay curled up in a boxcar on a freight train heading for Chicago. It was a cold December morning in 1960, and I was eighteen years old. I had gone to sleep just hours before, and woke at the shrill cry of the train whistle. I came awake at once. You had to be on guard when you rode the rails. There was always danger from "yard bulls" looking to throw you off the train, and other hobos, poor as you were, looking to rob you of what little you had.

I loved the thunderous rumble of the freight trains. It was the sound of power. Watching the countryside roll by, I felt like I was finally controlling my own destiny. Every train north felt like passage into a new world. Despite the danger, I loved those smelly old wood freight cars, even those filled with livestock. Some trains, called "hotshots," carried butchered meat for next-day consumption. To avoid spoilage, they got to their destinations faster than regular freights. It didn't really matter to me how slow or fast they went, to me they were all carriage to freedom.

Chicago lay ahead, open as a naïve child. Even shivering from the cold, I sat contentedly in the corner with my arms wrapped around my legs. Every breath was a frosty cloud and I had to rub my hands together to keep up the circulation. Soon, the light grew bright enough for me to see through the cracks in the door. Whistle blasts told me we were stopping. I pushed the door open to look out. The wind froze my face, but surprising warmth ran through me. I was here. I had made it.

In the rail yard, there were dozens of tracks and hundreds of freight cars on the sidings. I was in Chicago, and I could see a cityscape of buildings rising like mountains in the distance. Chicago was different from anything I had ever experienced. There were no cotton fields anywhere. Skyscrapers lined every street and throngs of people crowded the sidewalks, holding their coats tight against the winter wind and darting in and out of fancy stores. Exhaust from the cars and trucks wrinkled my nose. A noisy mechanical plow rumbled through the streets pushing aside beds of snow. Trolley cars slid by with electrical connectors attached to overhead wires like shark fins, and telephone poles stretched ahead for miles.

So far, no one had called me nigger.

It was a good start.

I walked till I found myself on Cicero Avenue. Cold and tired, but so excited I could barely breathe, I put a coin in the pay phone on the corner and waited nervously for someone to pick it up.

After five rings, my aunt Shirley answered. "Hello?"

"Aunt Shirley, this is Richard."

"Richard, is that really you? How is everyone at home?"

"I'm in Chicago," I said, and she let out a shriek.

"You're here? Where are you?"

I told her and she said happily, "Stay there, I'm on my way."

The sound of her voice was a comfort. As I waited, my spirits couldn't have been higher. I surely was in heaven, the place I had dreamed of, where anything was possible, where the problems and hatreds of the South were far behind. At that moment, I didn't care about my dirty clothes or how much money I had. My thoughts were all about how here in Chicago I could finally find my own value, my own worth.

A big old Cadillac cruised by with a woman looking from one side of the street to the other.

I yelled, "Aunt Shirley, is that you?"

Grinning from ear to ear, Aunt Shirley parked at the curb and hopped out with outstretched arms. "Richard, I'm so glad to see you. When did you get off the bus?"

"I didn't take the bus, Aunt Shirley. I hopped a freight train," I said as she released her warm embrace.

"Richard, you should have told us you were coming."

"I kinda left in a hurry, Aunt Shirley." The truth was, my mom knew I was going, I just hadn't told her when. I wanted to spare all of us the sad and tearful scene it would have been.

"Well, let's go home and face your uncle. Is *he* gonna be surprised to see *you*," she said jokingly.

I got into the car. Two children were sitting in the backseat. "Richard, this your cousin Franklin and your cousin Penny."

"How you doing?" I said.

"We all right," Franklin said, as his sister buried her head in his chest shyly. "You gon' stay with us?"

"I hope so," I answered.

The little girl examined me closely. "Why is your nose so big? It looks swollen. When's it gonna go down?"

We drove the rest of the way in silence.

Uncle Roman and Aunt Shirley lived in an apartment on the west side of Chicago. Ten families lived in the building. Unlike the wooden dwellings of Shreveport, their building was dark red brick. The mailbox wasn't at the curb but was actually attached beside the front door. As we walked up the unbroken steps to the apartment, I asked, "Can I see the shower that comes out of a pipe and cleans you?"

Aunt Shirley laughed. "I know what you mean. When I first left the country and saw that thing, I was shocked 'cause I was used to bathing in a number-three tub."

The apartment seemed like a palace to me. There were three bedrooms, a bathroom, a dining room, and a living room. In the living room, two blue floral-print couches sat next to matching chairs. There were end tables with lamps, and a round table with ceramic figurines. A black-and-white television sat regally at one end of the room. The walls were full of family pictures, ceramic birds, and mirrors.

One wall held a big picture of Jesus. He was white. A Klansman once told me, "Jesus don't let little ugly niggers like you into heaven."

Aunt Shirley showed me the restroom. I had never used a toilet before. I didn't know how it worked. She had to show me to pull up the seat and how to flush. After looking at the shower, I asked, "Aunt Shirley, can I see one of your towels?"

I couldn't believe how soft it was. I rubbed it all over my face and hands. I must have looked silly. Aunt Shirley was trying to keep from laughing. Finally, she exploded. I joined her and we laughed until we cried.

Uncle Roman was surprised to see me when he came home. "Richard, does Julia know you up here?"

"No, sir," I answered, afraid he would be angry.

All he said was, "No matter. I'm glad to see you. Now let me wash up."

Uncle Roman was a construction supervisor. When he got home, his clothes, shoes, and face, were covered by so much thick white dust that he looked white. His large "white" hands looked tough and strong when he pulled off his yellow hardhat and vest. When he removed his dark green goggles, around his eyes were the only dark spots.

After Uncle Roman washed and changed, Aunt Shirley served us dinner at a long oval table with a lace tablecloth. She set plates, saucers, forks, spoons, knives, cups, and glasses, all a luxury to me. Uncle Roman sat at the head of the table like a king, and Aunt Shirley sat at the other end like his beautiful queen. Franklin and Penny argued over who would sit next to me. Penny won. Then Aunt Shirley set plates of hot food in the middle of the table, and the delicious aroma made my stomach growl. Kool-Aid was the drink of choice in Shreveport, but here they had real soft drinks.

After we said grace, I attacked the food like a hungry wolf.

"Richard, you had enough? Don't be shy. Eat as much as you want," Aunt Shirley urged.

Between mouthfuls, Uncle Roman said, "I'm happy you come here, Richard. You don't belong in the South 'cause you too damn stubborn and strong-willed, just like I used to be. I never got Julia to understand that. I wanted to invite you here but I would never go behind my sister's back. Whenever I discussed you moving here, Julia got so mad. We ain't never had nothing but struggle all our life. I couldn't understand why she wanted you to stay there to be a janitor like her, or maybe end up dead."

His face grew pained as he looked into the distance. "When I was about your age, some white men spotted me in the woods while I was hunting. They stood me up against a tree and tied my hands around it. They ripped my shirt off and beat me until the flesh ripped from my body. Every time that whip hit me, I screamed."

His eyes brimmed with tears. Aunt Shirley came from the end of the table and sat next to him, rubbing his arm compassionately as he continued.

"I remember asking God to let me die 'cause it wasn't nothing to live for. Then a voice inside my head kept saying, 'I'm a man. I'm a man.' All of a sudden, I didn't feel no more pain. Every time the whip cut into my skin, I whispered to myself, 'I'm a man.'

"They left me out there to die, but old Mr. Beaumont found me and took me home. Julia and Mama doctored on me until I got better. But the scars never went away, Richard. Every time I came to Shreveport I begged Julia to let you go home with me but she say no 'cause things wasn't as bad as they used to be. She'll be mad at me when she find out you here, but I'll deal with that. I might even be able to get you a job here. If I do, can you start right away?"

Hot food, nice apartment, family all around—and best of all, no Shreveport? I grinned happily. "Any time you say, Uncle Roman."

As good as his word, Uncle Roman got me a job, working with him. We reported for work at 7:00 a.m. in freezing temperatures, and left at 4:00 p.m. Aunt Shirley rose early and filled our brown lunch bags with sandwiches she made from dinner the night before, and cookies she baked because Uncle

Roman had a sweet tooth. He had a hot cup of coffee every morning but I never touched the stuff. Generally, I still don't.

Construction was new to me and I didn't know what was worse, the height or the cold. At the site, I saw right away why Uncle Roman's face and hands were always white. We spent most of the day lifting sacks of concrete mix up dusty ladders onto scaffolds and pushing wheelbarrows filled with sand. We froze all winter, something new to a boy from Louisiana. I don't think I have ever been so cold for so long. Coming home from a hard day's work was always a pleasure, because Aunt Shirley had the radiator on in the apartment and it wrapped us up in a blanket of warmth.

Although I adjusted to the work and the cold, and as much as I appreciated Uncle Roman's help, I knew I wouldn't be here long. Being a laborer was no better here than in Shreveport. I had a different goal in mind, to be in business for myself. I wanted to start reading again and, to that end, I was astounded to learn I was allowed to go to the public library. Every time I went, I checked out seven books. My goal was to read one every three days. Waking each morning at three-thirty, my reading marathon began. I even read during the thirty-minute drive to and from work, and every night from nine to eleven-thirty. I read books on business, business management, accounting, geography, and the few I found on black history. I read books of every kind and soaked up information like a sponge.

After three months, my commitment to reading had not faltered. My intellectual muscles were growing as fast as my physical ones. New horizons opened. I thought about enrolling in the Illinois Institute of Technology in Cook County. A degree would mean I'd be able to vote, something I had never done before. It wouldn't be easy to go to college. It was higher than

I ever thought I could aim, but I was used to dealing with obstacles, so I knuckled down even harder and read even more.

One night at dinner, six or seven months after I arrived, Penny asked me, "Uncle Richard, why do you read so much?"

"In Shreveport, it was against the law to go to the library. If you tried, they would beat you up and throw you in jail so nobody else would go, either."

She was amazed. "They beat you up for reading?"

"They figured, if you couldn't read, you couldn't vote. I want to make sure they let me vote. That's why I'm going to college."

Uncle Roman laughed. "Richard, in Chicago you don't have to graduate from college to vote. Once you old enough, all you need to do is register."

"Is that the only reason you wanna go to college?" asked Aunt Shirley.

"No, I want to be a businessman. I'm gonna make a difference in this world," I said.

I saw a flicker of something cross Uncle Roman's face that I couldn't identify. "Well, it's all well and good to have something you want to do," he said. "But you shouldn't give up a good job while you're doing it, should you?"

"Uncle Roman, I don't want to do construction for the rest of my life."

He frowned. "It's a good safe job. The pay's regular. Look around you"—and his arm swept around the apartment—"it got us all this."

That's when it hit me. The look in his eyes. I understood it. I had seen it all my life. It was fear. Fear of getting ahead. Fear of being equal. Uncle Roman accepted the idea he could never have as much as white people. Looking at his apartment, his life, it all seemed okay, but compared to what? Seen through the lens of Shreveport, he had a great deal—but compared to the white people around him, he had nothing. The realization crashed down on me like a load of the bricks we worked with every day.

If you live long enough, experiences begin to repeat themselves. That dinner table was the beginning of wisdom. Chicago was not like Shreveport—it was far worse. Chicago was an illusion. The best things here were just as inaccessible to black people as they were back home. Maybe it was worse, because we were told they were within our reach. In Shreveport, you couldn't go into the white museum or the white library. Was Chicago any better? Sure, I had access to libraries, but those in black areas were far less good than those in white neighborhoods. I realized that here black people thought they were free, but the same rules that applied in the South applied in the north. We still lived on the bottom.

Was this the promised land?

"You can even buy you a house up there," Uncle Roman had told me when I arrived. He was right. You could. But most of the houses blacks could buy were so dilapidated you could see through holes in the floor right down to the next apartment. You could see the sky through the roof. Where were the black businesses and entrepreneurs? What did it say that working at the post office was the best job a black man could have? You'd live and die carrying a bag for white people all your working life, *but at least it's secure 'cause it's federal.* All the hard work Uncle Roman put in at his job, hour after hour hauling brick and cement into those big buildings, was no better than picking cotton.

When Chicago people came to visit us in Shreveport, they all talked about how much they had. "I have three cars in Chicago," one claimed. In Shreveport we responded, "Wow, I just have an old mule. Maybe in Chicago, I could have three cars, too." I saw people who did have three cars, and some had even more, but they were mostly broken-down wrecks that would never run again. I had been so stupid. I'd never really looked closely at the car Uncle Roman drove. It could barely make it there and back, and a couple of times it broke down.

The truth was right in front of their faces. They just wouldn't see it. The police here hated us the same way, and beat us up the same way. The only difference was that the police here were more organized and could catch you quicker. Chicago had no ditches to jump, no woods to hide in. It was the same with food. Here, everything was in stores. It took money to eat. In Shreveport, we could always steal a chicken or pull food from the ground.

Segregation in Chicago was a fact. Racism was a fact. Separate schools were a fact. Ghettos were a fact. In Chicago, you were still called nigger. You were still beaten up. You were still shot. You were still poor. Even if you were doing as well as Uncle Roman and Aunt Shirley, white people could treat you any way they wanted to. They were the law. The pride that the North took in being so liberal and liberating black people from the South was the worst lie in the world because it could get you killed. It *would* get you killed.

In order for a lie to work, you have to believe it. I saw the truth. I wasn't about to live that way. I was so disappointed in Uncle Roman it broke my heart. He told me when I arrived I could do anything I put my mind to, but in the end he didn't really believe it. Did he *ever* think I would succeed? It made for a rift between us that grew worse every day and never healed, and soon I realized I had to leave his home and find a place of my own.

I had been paying Uncle Roman a sizable rent to live with him. I wanted to cut my expenses so I could send money home to my mom and my sisters. I moved into a cheap apartment on the west side of Chicago. It was depressing. Tenement buildings leaned against one another like drunks. I had never seen a neighborhood so disorganized, so filled with garbage, so filthy. In the hallway of my firetrap building, I daily passed people having sex, or doing drugs, and saw bodies sprawled out on landings or in the vestibule, unconscious or dead.

The apartment cost twenty-five dollars a week, but it wasn't worth a penny. The water pipes leaked. The old refrigerator never ran right. Bugs infested the kitchen. Rats feasted on garbage and lived in basements and bit people while they slept. In the hallway, I saw rats bigger than the rabbits I hunted as a kid. I was so afraid of being bitten, I couldn't sleep. I lay awake at night while the rats scurried inside my walls.

A week after I left Uncle Roman's, I got a job working in the mailroom of a big commercial office building in the Loop, Chicago's downtown commercial center and the seat of city government. It paid me $1.50 an hour. The office building was a welcome change from the construction site. No more overalls and heavy work boots; my new uniform consisted of dress trousers, a long-sleeve white shirt, and a bow tie, the first I'd ever worn. Feeling strikingly handsome and confident, I was sure I could work my way up.

Wanting the bosses to notice me, I worked harder than anyone. My energetic demeanor, however, disturbed some of my coworkers. One worker named Perry was a light-skinned Negro who had recently migrated from Huntsville, Alabama. Perry was the perfect example of a frightened Negro—no confidence, no courage, and no character. "Yes, sir," was his instantaneous response, spoken with a bowed head to any white man, careful never to look him directly in the eye. I despised his cowardice.

In the next nine months, I was promoted twice, so I wasn't worried when the department manager called me into his office one day, but Perry saw only darkness.

"I been here for two years and Mr. Hayes ain't never invited none of us Negroes to his office unless he's firing them," he said nervously.

"I won't be getting fired today," I said confidently.

The boss, Mr. Hayes, a tall, thin white man in his fifties, was a clerkish type with reading glasses perched on his nose. From his desk, he motioned me in.

"Sit down, Richard. I hear you do all your work and then help everybody else. I like that. I also hear you are a good basketball player, as good as the pros."

I looked directly into his eyes and he went on.

"We have a basketball team and I'd like you to play on it. Frankly, we're terrible and we lost badly last year. I don't want us to look like fools again. I spoke with the vice president and he agreed we can promote you. We'll pay you good money, too, if you play. How does $125 a month sound?"

"How does *$150* a month sound," I countered. "I'd love to play for your team if $150 sounds good to you."

He nodded grudgingly. "Let me talk to the VP and see what we can do. You can go back to work now."

Two days later, Mr. Hayes informed me that I would be paid $150 a month during the basketball season. If we won the championship, they would pay me *$200* a month, with another increase the following year. Having no faith in the legal system, I insisted the agreement be put in a written contract signed by all parties. They agreed. I couldn't believe it. Now,

I would be able to pay my rent, eat, *and* send money home.

Recruiting other black men from the neighborhood was easy. Going up against a "superior" white man's team was an instant draw. Mr. Hayes and the company got their money's worth. On defense, I shut the other teams down. On offense, no one could stop my hook shot. I averaged twenty-seven points a game and we won the championship.

As a result, my wardrobe became more stylish and fashionable, wing-tipped shoes, dress socks, pin-striped trousers with suspenders, starched white shirts, bow ties, and finally underwear, some of the first I ever owned. It was a new era for me. I was young, I was single, and I had money in my pocket. All that made me a very eligible bachelor.

That didn't mean as much to me as it did to most other young men. I didn't shun relationships with women, but I knew they could lead to problems. I found the women in Chicago the same as in the South, uneducated, compliant, and focused almost entirely on bearing children. They didn't know any better. Malcolm X said that "a man cannot do better until he learns to educate himself." Black women in Chicago were as poor as they were uneducated. They believed the myths passed down from generation to generation. They learned what their mothers told them, and their mothers had learned it from their grandmothers, all the way back to slavery.

I was ambitious. The women I saw around me and where I lived couldn't help me gain any of my dreams. To reach an understanding before I ever made a commitment with any of them, I was completely honest and took nothing for granted. "I know what you gain if you're with me," I'd tell them. "What do I gain if I'm with you?" Sadly, they were all the same. They had no vision of success other than working at some mindless job that offered nothing in the way of improvement for them or for me, and having kids. I didn't want to be involved in that type of relationship.

I asked my uncle what to do.

He told me, "You know that corner right there?"

"Yeah, I know where that corner is."

He said, "I go up there and get me a girl and have sex two or three times a month. That way I don't have no responsibility. You can do the same. If you don't wanna do that," he said, "the bathroom is in there."

Recreation was not always easy.

Even when it came to sports, certain areas were still closed to me. I had learned to play golf at a country club in Shreveport. Only white people could be members, but Negroes could earn a little bit of money working in the kitchen cooking and serving food, or tending the lawns and bushes, or caddying for members and guests on the golf course. As a young boy, I caddied for lots of people, including one guest member, a well-known actor named Dale Robertson who starred in Westerns. He liked my caddying so much he actually gave me one of his clubs, an old number-one iron. From the time I was about ten years old, I hit balls with that club. As time went on, I fixed a couple of discarded clubs and an old putter lying around the clubhouse until I had enough clubs to play the whole course. I could only play at night, but I was a natural athlete and, long after hours, I would roam the course. I got to the point where I was sure I could beat most of the members, but that was a dream I never realized.

In Chicago, blacks couldn't play on city courses so, for the fun of it, I used to borrow a friend's clubs and go to a nearby park to hit balls. I was out on a grassy area, driving balls across a field, when a well-dressed white man carrying a few irons approached me. I had seen him here hitting balls before, probably his after-work exercise. He was a big, dark-haired preppy sort with a flattop haircut, a big jaw, and blue eyes, in his midthirties, wearing a shirt and slacks. He carried his golf bag and a full set of clubs in the trunk of a beautiful two-tone '53 Buick Roadmaster convertible he parked in the little gravel lot nearby. I loved that car. It was salmon and beige and had those little chrome holes on the sides we called "Ghetto Bullets." I dreamed of owning it every time I saw it. The idea of driving up to Uncle Roman's apartment building in it made my mouth water.

He said, "You play golf?"

"I used to play golf," I told him.

"Are you any good?" he asked me.

"It depends on how you mean that."

He said, "You think you can beat me?"

I laughed. "Oh, yeah, it would be too easy, man."

It made him mad. "No, you can't," he insisted.

I waved him off.

He said, "I'll tell you what. If you don't beat me, I'm gonna whup your ass."

I said, "Well, okay, but if I beat you, I'll whup *your* ass."

His face got all steely hard. "It'll never happen . . . ," he said, and I swear I could hear the word "nigger" complete the thought in his head.

Of course, Preppie didn't know I had caddied from the time I was ten years old, or that I used to hit at least a barrel of balls with that old number one iron—not a bucket, a barrel—every week. I was just fooling around in the park, but this was a serious wager. He was big enough and crazy enough to try to beat me up.

I teed up a ball and hit it a mile. It soared straight into the sky and dropped into the woods at the end of the field. As soon as I hit that first ball, his jaw dropped. It didn't take any more than that to convince him he couldn't beat me. Right then and there, he started making noises about how maybe this wasn't really a bet and how maybe it wasn't such a good idea.

"Well, I'll tell you what, boy," I said. "Now, you better hit that ball. Or I'm gonna whup yo' ass."

"Well, if I don't hit a ball," he stammered, "there's no contest. No contest, no bet, right?"

I said, "Now, if you gonna hit that ball, hit it. You know that I'm gonna beat you either way."

"Well, I'm not gonna hit the ball," he said and turned to walk away.

I grabbed him, hit him, knocked him hard to the ground, and took his car. I drove it all around town. I was completely relaxed about the whole thing. I was so sure the car was mine, it never occurred to me it wasn't. See, where I came from, whatever white people took from you wasn't yours, it was theirs. There wasn't any need to call the police because they'd come and beat you. If the white man came and took your meal, it was his meal. If he took your pig, it was his pig. The time the sheriff took my kill, it was his kill.

I took the guy's car, it was mine.

You think that's crazy? No, sir. It was the natural order of things. I could already imagine driving the car back to Shreveport and visiting my mama and sisters.

When I got to my uncle Roman's house, he just looked at the flashy Buick, and me, in amazement.

"Man, you can't afford that car. Where'd you get it?"

"I took it from a white man. He lost it hitting golf balls with me."

Uncle Roman shook his head. "It don't work that way, Richard. The police gonna be lookin' for you in that car. You can't keep it in front of where I live at. Here's what we'll do. When it gets to midnight, we'll take the car and park it someplace else." He shook his head again and sighed. "That car will get you killed, Richard."

I didn't listen. I drove it around. I wasn't hard to find. Soon, the police stopped me. They had the license plate number from the report the man filed. The officer said, "If you don't give that car back, I'm gonna have to lock you up."

I still believed it was my car, even when they took it back from me and dragged me to the police station. Some of the policemen talked to me about it. They told me what I had done was robbery. That was the law.

Was it clear to me? they asked.

I said it was.

They said they were glad I understood. After all, the law was black-and-white.

CHAPTER **TWELVE**

No matter what promise Chicago had held for me, nothing had fundamentally changed. That included the attitude blacks had toward each other. Black-on-black crime in the inner city was on a rampage. Murders, stabbings, rapes, robberies, muggings, and beatings were an everyday occurrence. Like new enemies in an old war, blacks turned on each other with a vengeance. Black men pimped out our women on corners like slaves sold at auction. Others succumbed to drugs and addiction. We were a hopeless people divided not only by racism, but by the contempt we had for each other.

In my midtwenties, it suddenly became important to me to speak my mind. Hate inflated my being like a balloon filled with too much air, threatening to burst from the pressure. I was determined that black people in Chicago would listen to my calls for action about the lack of jobs, violence in the community, how black people were being abused, and how often we were innocent of the crimes white people charged us with. I was insistent, even when people told me change was impossible. They saw me as a troublemaker. I was warned there would be violence from white people if I didn't stop, if I didn't accept things the way they were.

Frustrated, wanting to make more money, and with the rats in my apartment keeping me up all night, I took a second job at a finance company as a "traffic manager," moving documents through the office. It was an opportunity to learn more about business, and the extra cash let me send more money home to my mother and sisters. I immediately began studying to take the tests to become a bookkeeper. I received help from a strange source. A homeless white man in my neighborhood, named Clifford, noticed my books and my studying. He offered to help me. I thought this strange, given our positions, but soon found out his sad story. He had been the VP of a small business. When he returned home from a business trip, he found his wife and children had deserted him. It tore his heart out and he took refuge in the bottle. He soon lost everything.

Clifford took delight in explaining bookkeeping and accounting to me. In his lucid periods, between half-pints of gin, I learned quite a lot. It was my first chance to test out some of my own theories on someone who had practical experience in business. Several times, I invited Clifford into my apartment to feed him and sober him up, but he would never come. He soon drifted out of my life, but I will never forget the help he gave me, teaching me things I still remember even to this day.

The head of the finance company I worked for was a white man named Mr. Livingston. He was well built, in his forties, with dark wavy hair, light gray eyes, and pockmarked cheeks. He always wore a dark suit, a white shirt, and a tie. Livingston prided himself on having the best employees in the company. When the results of my skills tests came in, I had top grades. I was certain he'd grant my request for a promotion, no questions asked.

I went into his office to speak to him. Mr. Livingston sat at his desk behind a stack of papers, fingers tapping calculator buttons as fast as a jook joint piano player. I hated how much I was afraid to confront him. He was just a man and so was I, but we lived in different realities. He had power and authority. I had none. There were no cotton fields here, yet facing him was like being in the fields all over again.

He looked up from his work. "Richard, why are you just standing there? Come on in. Have a seat."

I sat down. There was a picture of his white family on his desk, displayed like a precious trophy. On the wall was a copy of his college diploma. His green desk blotter was neat and clean, but cigarette butts overflowed his ashtray and the room smelled of them.

"What can I do for you, Richard?"

"Mr. Livingston, I feel I have done an excellent job here and deserve to be promoted. I want to have a bigger role in the company's operations."

He sat back and pursed his lips. "Why aren't you happy, Richard? You're a good little worker and you're doing a real good job, under the circumstances."

"Mr. Livingston, I'm taking college classes in business," I said proudly.

"Richard, I know you're very bright. I noticed you've already taken all the tests required for being a bookkeeper, including some of the upper-level math tests."

"Yes, sir, my grades were the highest."

Mr. Livingston pulled out a folder from the pile on his desk and looked through it, nodding. "Your grades were higher than almost anyone. We'll have to see."

"Someone made better grades than I did?" I asked, knowing no one had.

"Well, let's take a look," he said, and shuffled through the pages.

No one outscored me on the test. I knew it, and he knew it, too. His guilty look told me so, as he flipped the pages without really looking. Then, I heard it.

"Bozo," he muttered under his breath. He said it like there was something I didn't get.

"Sir, what did you say?"

"Oh, nothing," but the word had already slipped out.

Where I came from, "bozo" was a pejorative nickname for black people, meaning a stupid clown, a fool.

"Sir, is there a particular reason why you called me Bozo?"

He kept his face buried in the folder and said nothing, but I knew. I wasn't going to get a promotion no matter what my test scores were. I rose to my feet and walked out of his office. My gullible expectations had resulted in a slap in the face.

Walking home that afternoon, my ghetto neighborhood reminded me of a portrait of the Old South. Women young and old wore stocking caps and tied rags around their heads. Men wore heavily soiled clothes and children played nearby, just as torn and dirty. Newspaper covered windows where windowpanes should have been, doors hung off hinges, drooping into the snow as if the cold had killed them.

There was no welcome committee here, not even a welcome person. I was not superman; I was a comical Negro who foolishly dreamed of ways to change things. I had misread the city completely. In this moment, I heard my mom's warning. "It don't matter where you go, Richard, things gonna be the same."

She was right. I just hadn't listened.

I left the ghetto and walked down the quiet streets of a nice neighborhood. The white residents noticed me immediately. I felt my dark skin create tension, saw them run to their phones. It wasn't long before a beat cop stopped me. He was average height, with a ruddy face and thick eyebrows, jet-black hair, and dark brown eyes. My eyes fixed on his black boots, perfect for kicking me in the head.

He put his hand on the butt of his gun. "What are you doing in this neighborhood? Do you have any identification? Where do you work?"

It wasn't the first time the police had stopped me and wanted to search me and move me along like a herd animal. "Is there a problem, officer?" I asked.

"Are you from around here?"

"I'm from Shreveport, Louisiana," I said.

He looked me over from head to toe. "You need to get your black ass back to Louisiana, boy, 'cause white people out here don't like poor niggers like you roaming their streets. Before long, somebody's house will be broken into or a white woman gets raped. All kinds of violent things have a tendency to happen when a nigger's around. You know what I mean?"

"Yes, sir," I said through gritted teeth.

"Do you know anybody in this neighborhood?"

"No, sir."

"Then get out before I put your black ass in jail."

"But you don't understand the reason why I'm here," I said.

He slid his hand around his gun butt. "I don't need to understand why. If you don't get out of here I'm gonna put my foot right up your ass."

I walked away calmly, contemplating what my next move would be. But he followed me and, not two minutes later, stopped me again.

"Are you trying to be funny?" he demanded.

"No, I'm not trying to be funny. Do you think I'm trying to be funny?" I asked.

His mouth tightened. "You walk around here with your head stuck up in the damn air like you own Chicago or something. Like a big shot. You better walk like you should, with your head down, or you'll find my foot not only in your ass, but all up the side of your head. Do you need me to kick your ass?"

I was so tired I couldn't stand it anymore. If just one more person pushed me around, I felt I would die. It was the same as the night in Shreveport when I couldn't take the abuse one minute more. I couldn't stand one more minute of bowing. It was too much to carry the weight of discrimination one minute longer. Standing in front of that cop, it wasn't enough to *think* the unthinkable; I had to *do* the unthinkable. From now on, I'd be the first to win, or the first to die. It didn't matter anymore. My bottom lip quivered uncontrollably and angry tears rolled down my face.

"Nigger, is something wrong with you?"

Even if tragedy came from this and I lost my life, I would walk right up to the valley of death without fear. Of one thing, I was certain. I would not, and could not, look down anymore.

The cop leaned closer angrily. "You been standing there for over a minute looking at me like a fool. Cat got your tongue, boy? Don't you hear me talking to you? Do you know who I am? I'm the police."

I shook my head slowly. "Officer, all my life I been giving white people all the respect in the world. It was undeserved and unearned, but I gave it. I ain't got no respect for none of you, and if you try to hurt me today, we both gonna die. I don't give a damn one way or the other. I will not lower my head like a scared fool."

"You think you own these streets, boy?"

I drew a deep breath and let it out slowly. "As far as I'm concerned I own all of Chicago. I own America, too, which gives me the right to knock your head off your body if you fuck with me. Now, you can go your way and I'll go mine, or we can stand here and fight until you kill me or I kill you. I will not be intimidated or insulted by you, and if you push me, I will push back."

He took a step back and drew his gun. "Nigger, step over to the car right now and shut your goddamn mouth before I knock your teeth out. I'm gonna search you to make sure you're not carrying anything. Face the car and put your hands up."

I was in too far to back down. Pulse racing, I said, "I have no reason to step to your car for a goddamn thing and you have no reason to search me. I've done everything I could to avoid a confrontation with you, but if it's a confrontation you want, you got one. The only thing I plan to do is walk home, unless you insist on one of us dying here."

I believe that that was the most important decision of my life. Even death was better than living another day in fear. Forced to choose between two evils, I would still end up with evil. There was no more escape. There was no more hiding.

Another black-and-white Ford police car pulled up and white officers jumped out with guns drawn. One went behind me and the other stood beside the cop who faced me.

He said, "I see you done caught yourself a nigger, Joe."

I cut in, "He might have caught a nigger, but he caught one that don't want a bunch of bullshit. I don't have time to mess around. I don't have time to stand around. I don't have time to be kicked around. By the way, my name ain't nigger. My name is Richard Williams. Don't call me a nigger again."

From this point, it's unclear what happened. When I woke up, I was in jail. My head ached and felt so heavy I was unable to hold it up. Fuzzy at first, it took a few minutes to focus. The index finger on my right hand was broken. There was excruciating pain in my ribs when I breathed. I felt bandages wrapped around my head, sticky with blood.

"Jailer! Jailer! Jailer!" I yelled at the top of my lungs.

I heard the jailer's voice before I saw his face. "Boy, what you want?"

"The last thing I remember, I was talking to the police. You let them know that I'm gonna be looking for them, and when I find them I want them to kill me. I made them a promise this would never happen to me again; never ever."

They kept me in the cell for two days. After my release, my number-one goal was to locate the officer who had first stopped me. I walked back to the same neighborhood I had been warned to stay out of. I walked the streets with my head high, dignified. Several officers passed and looked, but oddly enough, I wasn't stopped.

"I'm gonna challenge the person who beat the hell out of me and broke my ribs and busted up my head," I whispered to myself.

My search continued for several days. Finally, my prayers were answered. The same officer had the audacity to stop me again. At first, he didn't recognize me, but when he realized it was me, beads of nervous perspiration formed on his face.

I said, "You tried to kill me. I told you the first time you stopped me I wasn't taking no bullshit from you."

I plowed into the officer with all my might. Punching like a man possessed, my first blow landed in his mouth. Before his partner reached us, I got that sucker down on the ground and bounced his head like a ball. The other officer put a choke hold on me. Gasping for breath, I released my hold. Somehow, they managed to cuff me and threw me into the police car. I don't have to tell you what happened. I got beat up again and put back in a cell. They wanted to charge me with attacking a police officer. I didn't care what I was charged with. My mind was made up. Every time they released me from jail, even if it was twenty years later, I would look for the same bastard. One of us was going to die. He would or I would.

While I was in jail, a black prisoner approached me about being a snitch for the police. "I gets paid good money for being the eyes and mouth of the street." He told me, "I think you'll be good 'cause they ain't never seen a nigger like you before. You gotta lot of courage, man. If you stop being so hostile you could make some nice change."

I was on his ass like gravy on rice. I beat the living hell out of him because he treated me like an Uncle Tom. Did he believe I would sell out my people for a few dollars? There comes a time when every black man will be confronted with racism, because it's not a trend; it's a way of life. It doesn't make a difference where you live, work, or play; the only difference is you better be ready to stand up for what's right.

When they released me from jail, I knew I had conquered something. It was fear. The real victory, however, would rest with my finding the police officer again. I sat for hours on the street like a bum, waiting for that cop. It was my new occupation. I wasn't going to back down to anyone ever again. I felt I had a responsibility to myself, to my dignity. Patient in my quest, I saw him while I was on my way to the store to buy a soft drink.

I yelled, "Hey, you, I been looking for you for almost five days. Why you hiding?"

He said, "Boy, you best go on. I whipped the hell out of you twice. Next time I'm going to kill your stubborn ass."

Undaunted, I said, "Sir, that's the same promise I make you. Today, one of us will die. Either you beat me to death or I'm going to beat you to death. Your partner's not in the car now, so it's you and me, one on one. Get your gun out and shoot 'cause I'm coming at you."

He was nervous, his hand trembled, but his gun stayed in its holster.

"Boy, let, let me tell you something . . . ," he began.

I cut him off. "If you call me *boy* one more goddamn time, I'm gonna take you down. My name is not boy. You know my name."

"Mr. Williams, I don't want no problems. Please, just go," he said.

It was the first time in my life that a white man called me Mister, but it wasn't any consolation. "No, sir. When we finish, one of us will be in the backseat of your police car unconscious or dead."

"Look, I called you Mister. I never called a nigger Mister before. What else do you want, man?"

"I told you. Today one of us is gonna die. We just need to decide who."

Refusing to take part in my drama, the officer went to his car and drove off like the coward he was. I will never forget the sound of his screeching tires as he sped around the corner on two wheels. The taste of victory was sweet. It was one of the most important days of my life, a source of pride forever. But it was just one battle. The officer would be back with reinforcements.

All day long, I walked the streets, waiting for them. My wait paid off. Two cops I hadn't seen before stopped their black-and-white police car, jumped out, and faced me.

The first said, "Son, let me tell you something."

Julia Metcalf Williams, my greatest hero.

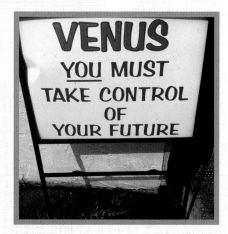

Signs posted around the Williams home and courts. "You learn a lot by looking and seeing."

Venus feeling the joy.

Always enjoying
the outdoors.

"Welcome to the Williams Show":
Richard proudly holds up the
sign prior to defending champion
Venus facing sister Serena in the
Women's Final in Key Biscayne, FL,
March 28, 1999. (Robert Sullivan/
AFP/Getty Images)

Richard defiantly clenches his fist
at the Tennis Masters Series final
between Serena and Kim Clijsters in
Indian Wells, CA, as he and Venus are
jeered by the crowd at the stadium,
March 17, 2001. (John Mabanglo/
AFP/Getty Images)

Richard practicing with Serena in 1991 in Compton, CA. (Paul Harris/Getty Images Sport/Getty Images)

Richard pushes ten-year-old Venus around in a shopping cart to make practice fun, August 1990. (Ken Levine/Getty Images Sport/Getty Images)

Teaching the serve to ten-year-old Venus. (Peter Read Miller/ *Sports Illustrated*/Getty Images)

Richard, Venus, and Serena at the Chris Evert Pro-Celebrity Tennis Classic, 1992. (Alese and Morton Pechter)

Venus and Serena (Alese and Morton Pechter)

Richard gets a kiss from the girls, 1994. (Alese and Morton Pechter)

Venus and Serena at the Virginia Slims Championships, 1994. (Alese and Morton Pechter)

Richard, 1994. (Alese and Morton Pechter)

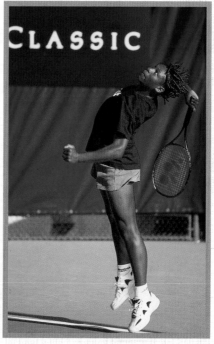

Serena on the court at the Acura Classic in Manhattan Beach, Los Angeles, 1995. (Alese and Morton Pechter)

Richard teaches his daughters—Serena (top) and Venus (bottom)—how to golf. (Alese and Morton Pechter)

I cut him off. "By now you know my name isn't son. You better call me by my name before I jump on your ass."

"Richard—"

"My name is not Richard. It's Mr. Williams, to you."

The officers exchanged glances and the second one shook his head. "Mr. Williams, I have a great deal of respect for you. We're not asking you to lower your head. We just want to avoid any problems with you 'cause we realize you're a crazy—"

"*What?*"

"Mr. Williams, what I mean is your way of thinking is different. You don't mind dying, it seems."

I said, "I'm here to die."

The officers got back into their car without saying a word. I knew then that dignity is not something you're given—it's something you take. You have to realize you can overcome barriers, face challenges, if you won't allow anyone to hold you back or keep you down. I did not accept control resting in the hands of people like these cops, or a man like Mr. Livingston. They wanted me to believe I didn't count, didn't matter. Instead, I took action.

Yet, there was a price. A steep one. Even now, those days in Chicago, and the beatings, come back to wake me in the middle of the night. My wife will stir and ask me what's wrong, why did I get up? I tell her it's okay, and I cover up the pain that never goes away, the pain of those fists and boots and the heart they took from me that still disturbs my sleep and robs me of peace of mind.

For all that I had won that day, I knew in my heart it was time to leave Chicago. I didn't belong there any longer. It was just as racist and backward as Shreveport, masked by skyscrapers and a notion of civility. Negroes found no favor there, only unemployment and crime among the tall buildings. It was a ghetto of despair and unfulfilled hopes. Sadly, I saw my own people as equally to blame. They bought into success as it was defined by the white man. They accepted his restrictions and limitations. Uncle Roman was a perfect example. He even told me how much he resented my rebellion against the police.

"Richard, word on the street is you been having a lot of problems. People are worried there's gonna be trouble stirred up. Son, don't start something with the police you can't finish."

He told me the police contacted him regarding my whereabouts and were looking for me. I resented his reluctance to support me. To me, it was not a matter of right or wrong; it was a matter of black and white.

I told him a big lie. "Don't worry, Uncle, I found a much better apartment and I'm gonna move again. My job is going very well and I'll be getting another promotion soon."

I couldn't love a man who had no courage. He looked ugly. He sounded ugly. He was just one more Negro afraid to stand up for something. The ironic part was that soon he would have to. Chicago was about to gain national attention when local civil rights leaders launched two citywide school boycotts to protest school segregation, overcrowding, and the use of trailers as facilities. Protest marches on City Hall caused police intervention and mass arrests. Maybe the police knew it was coming, maybe that's why they didn't kill me. It would have been one more log on the fire that was threatening to spread everywhere.

Chicago did become a battle zone. Martin Luther King, Jr., himself participated in two civil rights marches into all-white neighborhoods protesting segregated schools and the city's slums. Later, during a march through Cicero, a working-class white neighborhood, the National Guard had to be called in to protect demonstrators from whites and Nazis. The *St. Petersburg Times,* September 5, 1966, vol. 83, no. 43, carried a vivid description of it.

Violence Marks March in Cicero

National Guard troops fired into the air and jabbed white hecklers with bayonets as they fought off a mob seeking to attack some 250 civil rights demonstrators who marched through Cicero.

A crowd of over 4,000 white hecklers brandished white paper broadsides printed with a swastika and the words, "White Power." Although Cicero officials said that any members of the American Nazi party who showed up would be arrested, the swastikas were passed out in advance of the march and Eric Himmler, executive secretary of the Nazis in Chicago, moved about unhindered.

"I've never seen such savages in all my life," said Mrs. Ruth Huey who, with her husband, marched at the head of a column. Their son, Jerome, 17, was beaten to death in May by four white youths in Cicero and the site of the assault was a stop on the march route.

Three explosions as the marchers passed the intersection of Cicero Avenue and Cermak Road seemed to trigger the white crowd, which had grown to 4,000. Bricks, bottles, stones, and firecrackers fell on the marchers as they marched eight abreast down the street.

My mother had told me America was the same everywhere and that certainly seemed true. I was tired and disheartened. I gathered the money I had saved and sold everything I owned. I had left Louisiana almost five years before with little but the clothes on my back. I was leaving Chicago older and wiser, with money in my pocket.

My plan was to go out West, but first I had to do something I swore I'd never do again.

I had to go back to Shreveport.

CHAPTER **THIRTEEN**

I was once interviewed on television and the host asked me, "Richard, how does it feel to make a million dollars?"

I smiled. "Sir, I made a million dollars when I was sixteen."

He was quite surprised. "You were sixteen and you made a million dollars?"

I said, "I sure did."

He said, "Man, I thought you grew up in the Deep South."

"I did," I agreed.

"Then how did you make a million dollars?"

I laughed. "Hell, I made more than a million. I know it because I worked for white people who kept buying big plantation homes, big fields, big cars. Matter of fact, they bought the whole damn city. Sure, I made millions. They just kept my share."

*   *   *

Heading back to Shreveport, after my years in Chicago, was a time for deep reflection. Shreveport had been my whole world. I hadn't been anywhere before I left. Now, I had lived in a big northern city. What had I discovered? The world hadn't changed. The racial hatred I knew as a child was no different. What had changed was me. I was going back to Shreveport with money I had saved and the pride in myself that it created. The two jobs I had worked for over five years—and a third on weekends—let me save up enough to think about starting a business of my own.

The other important change came from college. Education changed the way I thought and acted. Besides a knowledge of business and books, I learned a greater degree of self-control. I learned how to stay out of fights. Instead of talking back to people, I learned to turn my back. I had a more mature understanding of people and their ways. I could still best them, but by turning the table on their arguments rather than by hitting them with the table.

I am a thinker. I try to understand everything. As I approached Shreveport, I realized I had had no respect for anyone as a child, including myself. My pain and hatred were so great I was willing to die. I think I *wanted* to die. Now, I wanted to live. I was still at war, but I could see my situation without the rage I used to carry. The one thing that never did change was my quick temper. To this day, I am quick to flare up and slow to cool down.

I understood myself better. I listened better. I left Shreveport a frightened boy. Coming back, was I a man? I should have been able to consider myself a man. I was over twenty-one. I had made money. I had sent money to my family. Yet, those things were true from the time I was seven. The truth was I never felt like I was a man in America, then or now. I felt like what the white people called me, an insult I still feel the pain of today. I felt like a nigger. I still do.

Heading back to Shreveport in 1965, lulled by the rhythm of the rails in that old boxcar, I knew I hadn't lost my anger despite all I had learned. How could I? From the day I left my mother's womb, I got the pounding of psychotic names like *nigger* and *boy*, and got beat up, and saw my father run in cowardice from an angry white mob, leaving me behind to be beaten. Despite my achievements, a racist America defined me then and now.

People claimed the first wind of hope for Negroes was blowing across the nation.

I didn't trust it.

The only thing I was going back for was the opportunity to tell Mama I was sorry for leaving without her permission, to apologize for not taking her advice about Chicago, and to ask for her blessing before I left again. I had to tell my family and friends the truth. Don't go to Chicago. It's not as bad as Shreveport—it's worse. It was pointless to worry about the Ku Klux Klan. Klansmen were everywhere. It was not a theory, it was a way of life. It often seemed to me that the only freedom to be found in life lay within the chilly hands of death.

It was a grand homecoming when I walked into our house. My mom was overjoyed to see me and threw her arms around me and cried. I told stories to her and my sisters, and ate with them, and slept. But by the next morning, I was restless. I wasn't going to leave without shaking things up. I felt a mission stir within me. I wanted to get black people in Shreveport to change their way of thinking, to acknowledge they were more than worthless niggers.

In a small neighborhood like Cedar Grove, news of my arrival traveled fast. People came over to wish me well, but the more I talked about civil rights, the more my renewed reputation as a troublemaker spread. I was in a dangerous position. I was alone and vulnerable. I heard there had been a black dentist on the other side of town who talked the same way I did. The Klan burned down his office and ran him out of town. My mom told me I had an uncle about fifty miles away who was also talking civil rights, but we never did get together.

I started stopping white people in the street and asking them questions about black people. "Do you think that blacks will ever go with white people to the same church, the same school? Can you ever see a black man marrying a white girl? Do you see a white girl ever marrying a black man?"

They looked at me like I was out of my mind. Even black people wondered why I asked those questions. My mom told me that Mr. Macey, the usually friendly manager of the A&P market, came up to her with a very worried expression.

"You know how much he likes you and loves you, babe," she said.

"Yes, ma'am. I do."

"Well, he told me that you asked him, do you think that a white girl one day will openly be having babies with black men and nothing will be done about it?"

"I did ask him that," I said.

"Well, he said you gotta stop asking questions like that. It's too dangerous. Why, they won't even let me shop at the market now."

"But why?"

"He was afraid you gonna end up raping a white girl. He said that if you don't get outta here you gonna not only get killed, you gonna end up kidnapping a white girl, raping her, and killing her, and definitely be hung in the middle of town."

Was it crazy? Not to him. Within the realm of his expectations, a black man talking about having sex with a white girl could only end in rape. One white man came up to me when I was asking those questions and told me, "Son, it's gonna happen someday, but I won't be alive to see it, and neither will you."

I caused trouble on all sides. The white community despised me because I refused to accept inferiority. The Negro community resented me because they feared my fight would cause them problems. As if I were a magnet, trouble followed. As I stood in line in People's Market on East Seventieth Street, an ugly white man wearing a Confederate T-shirt held up a box of pancake mix with a picture of Aunt Jemima on it and said, "Hey, Sambo, instead of teaching them niggers how to be self-sufficient, you need to teach them how to work for us." He walked to the counter and continued, "Y'all ain't gon' never do nothing but work them goddamn fields, where you belong."

Instead of getting angry, I tried talking. "Do you believe one day there won't be any more prejudice?" I asked calmly.

He became extremely angry. "Why do you think a clean race like ours would contaminate ourselves with you dirty bastards?"

"Do you think a day will come when blacks and whites will go peacefully to the same school, together?"

"Over my dead body. I would never let my children go to school with a coon."

Persistent, I followed him outside. "Do you think blacks and whites will go to church together?"

He answered angrily, "I don't serve a nigger's God. I don't even like living in the same city with you niggers. I don't know one white person that wants to live on the same street 'cause you stink and you're good for nothing."

I had not failed to see his four friends, who had hunting knives strapped to their belts, begin to circle me. I was no match for them. I was back in Shreveport, in danger again. So I did what I had learned to do so many years before.

I ran.

I heard them yell, "Catch him 'fore he get away. Let's make an example out of that little Chicago nigger."

I turned the corner of Seventieth and headed onto St. Vincent going south. I went in the back door of the drugstore, the official Negro entrance. After ten minutes, I saw their truck go by. Across from the drugstore was a bicycle store. Three beautifully painted brand-new bicycles with FOR SALE signs on them were parked on the sidewalk. I got on one and rode away.

As I rode home, I realized it wasn't safe for my mother and sisters for me to spend even one more day in Shreveport. White people hated me for trying to organize my race. Black people hated me for trying to organize my race. I endangered the hateful peace. Both sides thought the same, and I couldn't change their minds.

Before I could set one foot in the house, Mama was at the door.

"Richard, I heard you were running. Are you okay?"

After I shared the details, and apologized for worrying her, she said, "I wasn't worried at all. I knew if you got a head start, it would be impossible to catch you. No one can catch you when you running."

"I know, Mama."

She tried to choke back her tears, but they flowed from her eyes. She hugged me and said in a very gentle voice, "You can't change these people, 'cause they been down so long they don't recognize up. This place is no longer your home. I think it's best you leave 'fore you end up getting killed. I want you to get out of Shreveport. I'm gon' pack some food for you tonight and you'll leave right after dinner while it's still dark."

She was right. You cannot help people who do not want help. This time I would listen. I had her permission to leave, her blessing, understanding, love, and kindness. That night after dinner, we all prayed. As I collected my belongings, my sisters begged me to stay but Mama assured them it was best for me to leave. We all walked to the back porch. I picked up my clothes sack and Mama's box of food and strapped them to the bicycle.

"Where do you think you're going with that bike?" Mama asked.

I said, "I'm going to California, and the way I feel I think I can ride this bike all the way."

Mama smiled. "Maybe you should take a bus, Sonny."

She said good-bye and hugged me and cried, and my sisters did the same. I left them and rode down the dirt roads on the outskirts of town. My heart ached because I was leaving my family, but I was glad to be leaving Shreveport. As I rode, I tried to store a vivid picture of Shreveport in my mind. Three old black men sat on the front porch of a jook joint drinking wine like water. Intoxication was their refuge in a crazy world. I turned down a dirt road lined with old wooden houses with oilcloth shades and tin roofs. Fallen planks left gaping holes in the walls. Some slanted as if ready to fall over.

Tattered sheets hung outside windows and flapped in the night breeze. Curiosity got the best of me and I stopped by a window and peeped in. A man, three women, and five children lay asleep on the floor. A foot-tub full of dirty dishes sat in a corner with bugs floating on top. A dirty pot on the stove was filled with maggots. As I walked by, the breeze spread the rotten smell seeping from the outhouse.

I had wanted a lasting vision of Shreveport.

I got one.

My mother had told me to take a bus, but I headed straight for the freight yard and dug up my money, buried there in case I had to get out of town fast. I looked over the trains that were ready to head out of the yard. All trains have markings that tell you their origin and destination. Quietly, I found one heading north. There was danger. If the freight-yard detectives arrested you, they imposed harsh punishments. They took your food and money and belittled you every way known to man. Then they took you to the sheriff, who made you work on a road gang for several days until you were released.

Martin Luther King, Jr., was leading the fight on a national level, but in the face of the violence against black people, I found it difficult to embrace his views on nonviolence. I saw the dogs and the water hoses on television news. I saw the marchers keep on coming. Could I be knocked down repeatedly without retaliating? I was never good at it, but for once, I decided to try.

I decided to postpone heading west and go instead to Mississippi. I knew a man who was working on civil rights projects there and I wanted to join him. A series of freights led me to my friend and I joined his group working to register blacks to vote. Every day we faced threats and acts of violence. When a group of us went into a black neighborhood to talk to people about voting, a small crowd of whites intercepted us. They had bats, bottles, sticks, and bricks and kept calling us niggers.

I remember kneeling and praying to God for strength to get us out of there. While I was kneeling, a white boy pulled out his penis to urinate on me. I carried a homemade zip gun in my pocket. As I pulled the gun out of my pocket, one of our youth leaders rushed to my side and told me to put the gun away.

I said, through gritted teeth, "I'll shoot him if he pisses on me."

Fortunately, we were able to escape without injury, but I was asked to leave because I promoted violence. I knew it was true. I could not embrace a turn-the-other-cheek philosophy. I wasn't running anymore. "An eye for an eye and a tooth for a tooth" was my motto, and I insisted on living by it. I could not, and would not, be a victim again, not of my own free will. King and Malcolm X and Stokely Carmichael and other leaders of the civil rights movement had brought a new way of walking, talking, and thinking. It was time to be proud of our blackness. We had something to give to our community, to our city, state, and country, to the world. White people had better get ready for those of us willing to stand up for ourselves.

All around me, people claimed the wind of hope for Negroes was blowing across the nation.

I still didn't trust it.

No matter how much I would have liked things to be different, I believed the greatest civil rights victory I could achieve would be my own success.

It was time to live free, be free, and go into business.

Realizing no one could stop me except me, I hopped the first freight I could find and headed for California.

CHAPTER **FOURTEEN**

By the mid-sixties, it was hard not to see, even for me, that a certain level of change had occurred in black America. Although I had rejected the nonviolence philosophy of Dr. King, the man himself empowered me. In some ways I felt I understood him. I had taken all the beatings the white man could throw at me and not given ground, and Dr. King's message that a man without a dream is a man without a future was very appealing. I, too, believed that if we stopped dreaming, we closed our minds to the possibilities of tomorrow.

With my dreams in hand, I hopped off the freight train on the outskirts of Los Angeles. I had a plan. First, I would raise my level of education. Second, I would start my own business. My value would be what I created. I would live by my own judgment. I would accept no limits. It also made sense to work for myself because I could never work for anyone else for very long.

I had some distant family in the LA area, a very nice lady named Mary Alice Phelps, who taught at Pepperdine, a Christian university in Malibu, and her husband, Bill. Bill picked me up at the depot and took me to stay with them in Compton. Soon, the Phelpses' house became my base of operations, and I moved around the area learning what was going on in the neighborhoods and looking for a job.

Right away, I saw the deep-seated crime and corruption in Compton, but I ignored it. I was California dreaming. From the moment I hopped off the train, I thought everything in California was bigger, better, and faster than anything I had ever seen. Downtown LA looked like a futuristic city to me with its glass buildings, expensive stores, and vast highways. Gigantic billboards advertising the latest movies lined the roads and almost blocked out the sun. The giant freeways amazed me. Their loops and turns made roller coasters in the middle of the city, and cars slid on and off them like ants flowing in and out of a nest.

The sun was warm. The ocean was a place of celebration. The beauty of the water and the feel of the sand between my toes was a brand-new experience. I loved the gentle wind off the beach and the cool breeze on my face at night. I had never seen mountains before. Their size and beauty overwhelmed me. They, too, were bigger than life. One day, I wanted to be just as big. The idea drove me hard. I thought about it incessantly. I began to see opportunities. I had some money, but not enough to open my own business yet. I was self-educated, but had little formal education. As far as I was concerned, it would have been easy to rob, steal, and cheat, or to use racism as an excuse for violence. It would have been equally easy to become a slave to drugs or alcohol and slowly turn into a zombie like so many other black men. I refused. Life was at a crossroads, but I never was. Inside me lived an enormous desire to succeed that could not be detoured by the weakness other men displayed. It was that way with drinking. I am now seventy years old, but I've only had two or three drinks my entire life. Once, back in 1958, I took a drink and my mom took a broomstick and beat the living hell out of me. The lesson never left me. I didn't do drugs, because I had a cousin who was on drugs and I saw what his life was like. All he did was get high. He never knew where he was. He never owned anything. He didn't even care when he went to jail. I wouldn't allow that to happen to me.

Uncle Bill and Aunt Mary tried to get me to stay with them, but I always had to be independent. Never one to spend money easily, I rented a crummy old semiattached house on East Eighty-Eighth Street off Compton Avenue. It was a shack, really. The bedroom and the living room were all in one and extremely small. Compared to my apartment in Chicago, however, it was a step up. My bed was an old wind-up hospital type, but at least it was off the floor, and the walls had no bugs or rats. I didn't freeze in the winter, and during the summer I could ride to the beach on the old Humphrey bike I bought. The bike was my only transportation, but I didn't have to pay insurance or buy gasoline. Gas back then was fifteen cents a gallon, so I could save a few dollars a week. Most people don't save money like I do, but it is still the best way to create wealth ever invented.

Although I lived poor, I wasn't poor, but I wasn't ready to put the money I'd saved into a business. Unable to sit around and do nothing, I took a job at Buddy's Car Wash off South Alameda Street. Buddy was a gaunt white man in his thirties who drove a big Buick and loved to have sex with black women. I never liked him. When Buddy smiled, there was something sinister about it. Every time he looked at me, his cruel green eyes held hatred. I had seen those eyes before. They were the same eyes that chased me through the backwoods, eyes that lit up at the sound of the word "nigger," eyes that stared at me from inside a white hood.

I worked ten or twelve hours a day at the car wash, bored to death. The job was so repetitive I could wash a car with my eyes closed. I earned thirty to forty dollars a week, plus tips, and a few dollars more for pumping gas. The way it worked, when a car pulled into the wash bay, the tires depressed a steel plate connected by wires to a device inside the office that sounded a bell and recorded how many cars were washed. The clang of the bell was music to my ears, because it meant money in my pocket.

The car wash was a hangout for the bottom of society. Crooks, cons, and criminals made it their own. Prostitutes strolled in and out to use the restroom or get off their feet. Pimps drove in to show off their Cadillac Fleetwood Broughams, Eldorados, and Coupe de Villes. Their clothes were so fancy it looked like they were heading to a grand ball. The loved to smoke big cigars and brag about the women they had and all the money they made. The way they treated women made me as sick as the stench of their smoke.

The gang members loved to play a game they referred to as "Gas N Go." They'd fill up their cars and race off without paying. I put up with that for a while, till I decided enough was enough. The next time a pair of gang members gassed up and roared off without paying, I grabbed Buddy's car keys and a baseball bat and chased after them.

I followed them through the neighborhood at top speed,

foolishly ignoring the danger to myself and innocent bystanders. When they stopped and jumped out of their car, I stopped and got out, too.

"What you chasing us for, fool?" the driver asked me. "You stupid or something? Why you worried 'bout us hustling that white man's gas?"

"Why won't you pay for the gas, man?" I said. "Every time you steal gas, you taking money outta my pocket."

The gang member sneered at me. "You just one of those goody-goody niggers. You gonna get your ass kicked over that white man's gas?"

I shrugged. I was, and I did.

When I got back to the car wash, despite my bruises, Buddy cursed me out. "Richard, don't you ever take my car again to run after those boys. If they want to steal the gas, let them steal it. You damaged my car while you were out there acting like a fool. You know how your people are. They'll rob you blind if you let them. Now, go on in the men's room and clean yourself up and get back to work."

Regardless of my attempt to protect his livelihood, Buddy wanted me to pay for the damage I had done to his car. He told me he would take ten dollars per week out of my pay. It changed things between us. I didn't trust him as a man or a boss. I began to pay more attention to the way he was running the car wash and soon saw he was running an insurance scam, letting the gang members steal from him, splitting the take, and putting in insurance claims for the full value.

The longer I worked at the car wash, the more I began to believe Buddy was also selling drugs and fencing stolen goods. Worst of all, I suspected he was shorting our pay by falsifying the number of cars we washed. The trouble was it was hard to prove. I could never get an accurate count from him, and it was tough to keep tabs on a piece of paper in my pocket with my hands in soapy water all day long. I got one of those counters doormen use at nightclubs to count how many people are inside, and after a week or two I knew for sure. He under-counted the number of cars I washed by dozens every week.

If somebody cheated me, I had every right to cheat him back. The contract with Buddy was broken. All bets were off. Perhaps the smart thing to do would have been to quit, but I was never a quitter. Instead, I watched every move Buddy made. For a man who had no respect for black people, he had an enormous appetite for black women. Every day after work, I saw him cruising the areas where prostitutes worked the cor-ners. He couldn't get enough of the sisters. Some of the women came to the car wash looking for him. It turned out he was sell-ing them cocaine.

I continued to play the game of faithful, stupid employee. The deeper Buddy got into drugs and women, the more out of it he was, and the more he needed me to run things. Buddy told me quite often I was his best worker. By the end of the year, he told me he was making me the manager. The extra ten dollars a month was a joke considering how much he was cheating me out of, but the manager's position was the oppor-tunity I needed to get even, and I took full advantage of it.

I went down to see a welder I knew, named Melvin Thomas.

"Melvin," I said in his shop office, "can you make me two flat steel bars, at least four inches wide and fourteen inches long?"

He nodded. "Sure. Whatcha gonna do with them?"

I put money down on his counter. "Never mind. I just got to have 'em. Can you do it?"

"Just draw what you need on this paper," he said, pushing a sheet across the counter. "I'll make 'em right away."

We washed lots of cars during the week, but on Fridays, Saturdays, and Sundays, we washed ten times more. They all came through the car wash entrance, rode over the steel plate, and triggered the counter in the office. When I put the bars Melvin made for me over the steel plate, the cars didn't push it down so they didn't activate the counter. I smiled as I slid in those pieces of steel and ran a car into the wash to see if the bell went off. It did not. Car after car could roll through the car wash without a record of it.

The first week, I let just a few cars run over my anticounter device. I waited, testing my theory. Buddy didn't say a thing about it. One evening, after the car wash closed, I was locking up and I went inside to make sure the office windows were secured. As I snapped the locks, I saw two people in the alley. It was hard to make out their faces with the window so dirty, so I wiped it with a rag. I was shocked to see Buddy and a young black girl shooting up heroin. Buddy was heading for the bottom at increasing speed and bringing my black sisters down with him.

The next day, I confronted him.

"Buddy, for someone who dislikes black people so much, you spend a lot of time with black women. I saw you last night shooting heroin into your arm. The girl who was with you is only seventeen. She's just a child and you're gonna kill her with that junk."

He responded angrily, "That girl may be seventeen years old but she sure ain't no child, 'cause a child don't do the things with a man she does. You know what? I don't have to explain anything to you. You work for me and if you want to keep your job, you better keep your mouth shut and mind your own damn business. You can't save nobody. You're not Jesus Christ."

That week, I let twenty cars go through without being counted. Buddy had no idea what I was doing. He just kept doing drugs and screwing black women. It got to the point that any time Buddy was out, I disabled the counter and kept the money, sharing it with the other workers. In his permanent fog, Buddy just accepted that business was down and that was that.

"Buddy," I said to him one day when he was less high than usual. "We don't have nearly as many cars comin' through no more. Business is really slow. What do you wanna do? Close the car wash, or sell it?"

He waved me off. "I'm gonna leave it open. I been here for years."

I went into high gear. Buddy was going to pay for thinking me a fool. He would pay even more for contaminating black women with drugs. I now washed one car for Buddy, one car for me. A car wash was about a dollar, so I was making as much as fifty to seventy-five dollars a day. I once sent my mom five hundred dollars cash money. She sent it back with a note, "Whoever you robbed, give the money back."

By now, on average, we washed 250 cars a week. It went right by Buddy. He was so high he was in no condition to manage anything. Often, he lay in the alley like a homeless dog. I made up my mind to put him out of business. I began washing ten cars for me and one for him. Soon enough, he came to me complaining that business was not going well and he was planning to shut it down. I proposed to him that I rent the whole car wash from him.

He laughed at me. "Richard, I can't make a profit, what makes you think you can make any money?"

I just smiled and told him I felt in my heart I could.

Buddy agreed to let me rent the space for $250 per week.

He gave me a three-year lease with a two-year option to extend, and allowed me to work under his license and keep the business name. It was a happy day for me. I hired three employees and we made a big deal about welcoming everyone and promoting the car wash. In a few weeks, we were washing 110 cars on the weekdays at $1.50 per car. On the weekends, we washed as many as 250 cars. In addition to the car wash, we made three hundred dollars a week on the gasoline.

The problem was that once Buddy saw the place back in full swing, he didn't want to honor the agreement we had made. I had been renting the place for a few months by that time, and I thought about not giving the place back, but I knew it was never going to be a permanent business for me. The last thing I wanted to do was to spend my life working around gang members and pimps and criminals. Enough was enough. I gave the business back to Buddy. I figured he had repaid his debt to me and I watched from afar as the car wash slowly descended into what it had been before I got there.

I decided it was time to start working with my head, rather than my hands. In addition to the money I had made in Chicago, I now had the money from the car wash. It was enough to go into business. The only problem was that I had no idea what business to go into. I looked and I listened. I checked out retail stores and restaurants, real estate and public service. Information had always been the most important thing to me. The number of minutes I had to run so I could get to a safe place in Shreveport, the right farm to take cotton from, the ways to avoid female entanglements that held back so many black men. It turned out the natural fit for me was working in a bank—the place where money lived.

I applied for a job in the mailroom of the Citizens Bank at 453 South Spring Street in downtown LA, and was hired right away. I liked the bank and didn't feel pressured to move on, so I spent several happy years there. Life was good and I was learning a lot. I had an active social life and I had money—now deposited in the bank because after working there I believed I was close enough to it to deposit it safely.

It didn't take me long to see that most businesses—banks included—didn't know how to protect themselves from thieves. I saw how vulnerable the mailroom was, and how people were able to steal money with impunity. It was a real education, but it was nothing compared to what I learned next. Relationships often happen in the workplace, and I got very friendly with a girl at the bank. We liked each other a lot, and when she transferred to the data processing center a few blocks away, I applied to be transferred there, too.

Working at the data processing center was one of the best experiences of my life. I forgot all about the girl, and instead fell in love with IBM. I had never seen computers before. They fascinated me from the start. Back then, IBM computers were so big they took up half the room, and to input anything, you had to punch IBM cards with all your information on them. I was so captivated by them that even when my work was finished, I stayed late to learn how to use them. I watched people, asked questions, and saw that computers would soon become essential to doing business.

I learned how banks actually made money, how they made loans, what collateral was, how different kinds of bank accounts worked, how the personnel office functioned, even how they did their advertising and how they did their maintenance. In addition, I went to business school in Compton for almost a year and at night fell asleep reading every book I could get my hands on.

The dream of being someone, of making my mark in the world, burned hotter in me than ever. I was increasingly restless. I pushed myself harder. Despite my success, I felt off my mark. There was an internal pressure building up deep within me, but I was too driven to address it. I stuck to my program, sweeping aside the signs of what, in retrospect, I should have seen coming.

At Citizens Bank, I met a person who was pivotal in my life, an older white gentleman named Mr. Kelly. Mr. Kelly was an officer in the bank, and he took a fatherly interest in me, often telling me I should go into business on my own. He became a kind of private tutor, teaching me business, finance, and investments. We spent hours talking and he'd give me examples till he was sure I understood it all. The next night he would ask me questions. I had to answer every one of them correctly or he wouldn't move on to the next level.

Mr. Kelly was my patron saint. He encouraged me all the time. That encouragement was very important. I already believed in myself and had confidence. He made me feel my confidence was justified. Here was an accomplished man telling me all I needed was to be polished, like a diamond in the rough. When Mr. Kelly told me I should be in business for myself, I believed it.

I was familiar with the maintenance company that cleaned the bank at night, and the operation seemed financially sound and pretty simple. I decided I would open my own maintenance business. It didn't require much, just a clean record, not being locked up, not on drugs, and all that fit me well. I applied for a business permit and could barely believe it when I got it. I was so happy, till I learned I also needed a city license. It took a bit but I got that, quit the bank, and was ready.

I always believed in learning by doing, and I threw myself into my new business with enthusiasm. The thing I forgot, however, was I had absolutely no idea how to bid on a cleaning contract. I went around asking people in the business, *If you were bidding on a building and it was thirty thousand square feet and twenty thousand of it was office space, how would you bid?* When they wouldn't tell me, I tried to learn by looking and seeing. I went back to work for several businesses that hired companies like mine and saw how they ran their operations. I looked at their paperwork and saw what they were paid, and soon learned how to operate my business myself.

In 1967, I opened the White Glove Maintenance Corporation, duly licensed in Sacramento, California. I underbid several other companies for my first contracts because my total number of employees was one, me. My first job was a bank. I was afraid to work there at night because I feared someone might attack me to rob the bank. One of the managers laughed when I told him that.

"Richard, you won't have the keys to the vault or the safe-deposit boxes. You don't have a key to anything, except the front door. You don't have to be worried."

I soon had three businesses—the bank, a very popular café, and an insurance company. To save money, I did all the work. I worked as fast as I could on the first, then ran to the next, all night. But I wasn't content with just making a living. I wanted more. I had ambition. Pressure was still building inside me as I pushed myself harder and put money away, then pushed harder still. I kept it up until I had more money than I had ever dreamed of, but still wouldn't hire anyone to help me.

No matter that I had my own business and money now, I was still dissatisfied, extremely dissatisfied. I bought a second house on Grape Street in the Watts section of Los Angeles, then another in the same neighborhood, and rented them out. I'd ride out to the houses but I knew their value, even altogether, wasn't much, maybe forty thousand dollars. It was nothing compared to the homes of folks I knew in Glendale, a white neighborhood where black servants served the food and cut the grass. Their homes were worth $150,000 to $200,000.

I wanted a house on that level.

I knew a black doctor who had a beautiful house on the other side of the canyon from UCLA. On top of a hill, from his patio you could look back over to Encino and miles of beautiful homes. His house was worth maybe a half a million dollars. By comparison, I had nothing. The idea of not having a home in a rich neighborhood made me sick. I had come a long way from Shreveport, but still hadn't reached the level I wanted. I wasn't reaching the standards I had set for myself. It was like a cancer in my gut gnawing at me.

Despite that, coming to work with my mops, brooms, buckets, rags, and cleaning supplies gave me a feeling of accomplishment like none I had ever had. I had no limits but my own drive and ability. Soon, I had a long list of customers. By the end of the first year, I was grossing almost four thousand dollars a month.

With business booming, I needed more employees. My way of choosing them was far from traditional. Instead of going to an employment agency, I hired drunks from Skid Row. I wanted to give them an opportunity to get back into the mainstream of life and feel like human beings again. Each man had to agree to get off the streets and live with me in a big house I owned. As many as nine Skid Row associates lived with me at one time. They also had to agree to take classes and, most important, to stop drinking.

My intentions were good, but nothing prepared me for their alcoholic withdrawals. Some of them would shake so badly I thought they were having a heart attack or dying. On several occasions, I had to rush them to the hospital, where I learned their symptoms were part of the withdrawal process. I made a valiant effort to help them, but no matter how much I tried, before long, almost all ended up back on the street—with the exception of one: Hog Eye.

Hog Eye's real name was Master Benjamin David Hightower, the "master" provided by his mother to give him a rank the world would not. He was an articulate wino with a sophisticated air, even though he was also a stumbling drunk. He was about six feet tall but looked shorter because he walked with his head hanging toward the ground, and he had a distinctive voice that sounded like a bass drum, rich and round. He used to stagger down the street talking to himself in what we thought was a foreign language, but later learned was Shakespeare.

Hog Eye's fifty-year-old face was tired and worn, and a long scar lay across the left cheek of his French-vanilla-colored skin. One of his eyes stared back with no trace of life; it was a dead eye. Still, behind these things, you could see the handsome man he had once been. He had a presence that could not be defined by his outward appearance, and a special strength inside him just waiting to come forth.

Sadly, years of alcohol abuse and the treacherous life on Skid Row had taken its toll on his health. His liver and kidneys were in bad shape and it was almost impossible for him to get rid of a cold once he caught it. A former schoolteacher, Hog Eye used to help me teach his Skid Row associates. He taught with such passion and dedication that it was easy to see why he missed the classroom. Perhaps that idea was what stirred him to try to change his life.

One day, he came to me with a somber decision about his life and begged me to help him.

"Mr. Williams, I don't think I'm strong enough to stop drinking because I already tried that. So here's what I'm proposing. If you help me wean off the wine a little each day, then my body will need less and less alcohol. Before long, I won't need any at all. I'm not sure this is going to work but I'm willing to try because I want to see my family. I want to go home. My children are grown now and I have grandchildren. I want them to know they have a grandfather. I don't want anybody to tell them I'm dead. I know it'll be hard, but I know I can make it."

Hog Eye fought for his sobriety like a true champion. There were many bouts and devastating rounds, but he kept punching until he was able to get his life off the ropes. I kept him at my house and he continued to work for me throughout his ordeal. An avid reader, he continued teaching classes, but I was his only real student. We learned together. We laughed together. We ate together. We cried together and we prayed together. Hog Eye was a very intelligent and humble man. He was an engineer and loved jazz, classical music, and basketball. Sometimes we went to the park and played one-on-one. My youth and height were always an advantage, but even at fifty, he still had good moves. It was the first time in a long time he had felt like he was a part of something. It was the first time in a long time I felt like I had a friend.

Soon, sobriety unlocked the door of his prison and gave him his freedom. Hog Eye wanted to teach again.

"Mr. Williams, do you think I'm a good teacher?" he asked.

"Mr. Hog Eye, you're the greatest teacher I've ever known.

I've learned so much from you. I think our people have a lot to learn from you, too," I replied.

He rubbed his hands together nervously and paced back and forth. I had seen those gestures before, and for a moment, I thought he craved a drink. Then he explained, "All my life, I got picked on because of my light complexion. The dark-skinned blacks accused me of trying to act white. Other light-skinned blacks had no sense of belonging among their own people. But I was a great teacher. My students loved me, and I loved teaching them about who we were as a people and as a race."

He pointed an accusing finger at me. "Now, I'm not talking about the white man's version, because they wrote their own history. We were kings and queens, Mr. Williams. Nubian, Ashanti tribes, and the list goes on. But the white man won't teach that because as long as we think we're nothing we will always settle for second best. To be or not to be is the question. This day, I choose to be. I want to teach again and I don't just want a job in a high school. I think I have everything it takes to teach on the college level. What do you think, Mr. Williams?"

I had never heard him talk so long. Hog Eye made a great impression on me that day, talking about things no one had ever talked about to me before. Bear in mind, courses in black studies did not exist in most places at that time.

I said, "Any college would be making a big mistake if they didn't hire you, Mr. Hog Eye."

"That's all I needed to hear," he said, and rushed out with a smile on his face.

Hog Eye bought underwear, clothes, and shoes from the Goodwill. He cleaned himself up and started volunteering two nights a week at a local junior college. After three months of volunteering, the college asked him to teach full-time. He was open about his battle with alcoholism, and the college appreciated his honesty. As a result, they suggested that Hog Eye live in one of their dormitory apartments and also provided a meal plan. The final leg of Hog Eye's recovery was the day he went to Alcoholics Anonymous and announced, "My name is Hog Eye, and I am an alcoholic."

Hog Eye and I went our separate ways but always stayed in touch. He loved teaching and the students and faculty adored him. Eventually, I got a chance to meet his children and grandchildren. His beautiful family was extremely proud of him. I was, too. Whenever I sat in on his classes, he always made my presence known, informing the class I was his special guest. After his first courses were done, he signed a second contract with the college and eagerly looked forward to more teaching, but six months later Master Benjamin David Hightower suffered liver failure and died. I remember him still, an incredible man who taught me so much about having the will to fight.

I looked for more Hog Eyes out there, men who just needed a chance. I wanted to continue helping them. It was not to be. After Hog Eye left, I had four Skid Row associates living at my house, working for me. One night, on Compton Avenue and Eighty-Eighth Street, three of them got drunk and beat the fourth so severely he had to be rushed to the hospital, where he died. This incident was a turning point. I decided I would not try to rehabilitate the people on Skid Row anymore.

The years passed and my business expanded. I got new contracts and hired additional people. I bought trucks and equipment. Despite all that, cancerous thoughts were still growing inside me. I was successful, but I never felt like a success. I was trying my best to be a citizen of America, but I never felt like a citizen. I was twenty-seven but I had no peace. A new decade was approaching. I had accomplished so much. I was heading in the right direction. I should have been happy.

Instead, I was sure I was going to die.

I didn't know where it came from, but I couldn't escape the dire conviction I was going to die at twenty-eight. I was lost and confused. I was tired. Whatever money I had, and whatever properties I had, I couldn't bear the weight of them. I began to give them away. I gave away the houses. I gave away my money. I gave away almost everything I owned. When I turned twenty-eight, I think I had one pair of tennis shoes left and I would sit in my house alone, certain I was going to die.

A cop saved me.

Compton was a ghetto and violence was a part of daily life. You could be caught in the wrong neighborhood and end up dead. One night, a white police officer stopped me for speeding in a car I had borrowed from a friend.

"License and registration," he demanded.

I exploded. "I wasn't speeding and I'm not gonna take no nonsense from—"

He held up a hand and, surprisingly, spoke in a soothing manner. "Son, ease up. Wait a minute."

"I don't have to wait no damn minute," I shouted.

"Oh, yes, you do," he said, and looked at me curiously. "Son, do you *want* to die?"

I said, "No, I don't want to die."

He smiled. "Well, that's good, 'cause I'm not gonna be the one to kill you. You just go on your way, but I'll tell you this. If you don't change right away, you're *gonna* die, no question about it."

It hit me like a bolt of lightning. Suddenly, I knew where

the certainty I was going to die came from—it came from inside *me*. I didn't just believe I would die. I *wanted* to die. I had invented a way to escape my pain. Pain can build up in a man. It can be too large in him. I had lived with pain from the time I was a child and it finally built up in me to the point where I could no longer live with it. A man can only get so tired. His heart can only take so much. The list was too long. There was my father's rejection, my friends hanging dead on a fence or drowned in a river, my hopeless school, my bitter town, the spike in my leg, the cuts and bruises on my head and body, the life my mother was forced to lead, the fight to pull myself out of the hell white people made for me, and the running, always the running. I was in the prime of my life, but I was winding down like an old clock. It was ticking inside me every day. One more minute nearer to leaving. One more hour closer to release. Have everything, have nothing. Give it all away. Let it all go, and just die.

Surrender.

That policeman helped me a great deal because he started me thinking about my attitude. My problem wasn't the police, it wasn't any white folks, it was *me*. I had gotten so entrenched in the way I thought about things that I couldn't see anyone right but me. I looked at things as if everyone was trying to pick on me, or trying to do me in. No one was trying to do me in. I was doing myself in.

I was sure I was going to die, but I didn't. I kept on living. Of course, I had given away so much I had to start all over again, but it wasn't so hard. I was a different man now, with a different mind-set. I saw life differently. I knew how to restart the company, how to make even more money, how to face life without pressure exploding within me. I felt myself settle in for whatever life had to offer, with a more open mind.

I was back in business in a very short time, bought back what I had given away, and was able to repurchase my two homes soon after. It was time for another round of life, this time living it. But no one, not even me, could have predicted what was going to happen next, or the three things that changed my life forever—a beautiful young woman named Oracene Price, and two little girls named Venus and Serena.

CHAPTER **FIFTEEN**

Ambitious people drive themselves to lead. They're motivated. They have goals and self-esteem. It was easy for me to spot people without ambition. They were the ones without stress. They were the ones who give advice. *If I had what you have, I would do this. If I were you, I would do that.* They're not risk-takers. They never put themselves on the line. We should ignore these people because their advice never leads anywhere. They are the ones saying, "I know this person and I know that person."

Only ambitious people place their ideas before a crowd. The others stand in the crowd and look. Ambitious people may fear risk but they take it anyway. Love is a risk. Life is a risk. Ambitious people risk everything to find success, not only for themselves, but for their kids, their families, even their communities. To me, people who fail and file for bankruptcy are still ambitious. They are trying to try again. Failure is only short-term for them. Nonambitious people just walk away and don't even bother to pay the bills.

In the mid-seventies, I sold the White Glove Maintenance Corporation for a handsome profit and moved on. It was a hard decision but it freed me to pursue the kind of success I felt I had not yet attained. My savings account was larger than ever, but it wasn't enough. It was never enough. I was still adamant about not working for anyone else, so with the money from the sale of the company, I bought a cement truck and went into the cement business. I bought extra cement from construction jobs and sold it to companies building homes. I got it at a good price because customers had already paid for the cement. I also bought and sold cement from paving companies and paid their drivers to deliver it to my customers.

My next business was the security business. It was a natural for someone who knew as much about stealing as I did. To qualify for a license to open my own company, I first had to work twenty-four hundred hours as a security guard for someone else. I found a company just a block and a half from where I lived. The entire time I worked there, I only received one paycheck that was any good. The rest bounced.

I quit and went to work for a company located on Rosecrans Avenue and Aviation Boulevard, in Manhattan Beach. I rode my moped from Compton fifteen miles in the rain and fog to and from work, five days a week. The fog was very dangerous. One morning, I stopped at a traffic light and out of nowhere, a man grabbed my handlebars and tried to throw me off my bike. I hit the accelerator while fighting him off. The moped skidded through the intersection and I was almost hit by oncoming traffic. I didn't fare any better when it rained. On my way home, a car came up behind me and rode me up onto the sidewalk. I realized they wanted to jack me and take my moped. I dipped and dodged and finally escaped.

When I accumulated the necessary hours for my license, I opened my own company, the Samson Security Service. I proudly filed my corporate papers in Sacramento, California, and began to operate in different areas around Los Angeles. My main office was in Compton. If ever a security business was desperately needed, it was there. During the day, Compton was a peaceful enough place, but at night, all hell broke loose and criminals preyed on helpless victims. It was like the water hole in the jungle—all the animals came out at night to eat or be eaten.

No place was sacred. Robberies were everywhere. Criminals robbed churches, service stations, mom-and-pop groceries, banks, and even insurance companies. They became prime targets when they started accepting cash in their offices. Criminals also loved to hit construction companies because equipment and supplies were left on site. They were like supermarkets—so many items to choose from. Gangs stole commodes, sinks, doors, bathroom fixtures, copper wire, pipes, nails, bolts, screws, and windows. In some cases, after they robbed a site, they burned it to the ground to cover their tracks.

It hadn't taken me long to see that security here was a joke. Most places were protected by a guard who was so frightened he needed to be protected by another guard. The police were useless. No one called the police. It was no secret they were the most hated group in Compton. You never knew who they were going to beat up or drag off to jail once they showed up.

You'd think all this crime and chaos made Compton a terrible place to live. For me, it was a paradise. I applied what I had learned in the maintenance and cement businesses, and soon

I had contracts for several of the banks, office buildings, and construction sites in town. I had more than fifty men working for me and the formula was simple. The places we protected paid me twenty-four dollars per man per hour. I paid them eight dollars per hour, and after costs and taxes, had twelve dollars for myself, every hour my men worked.

I am about to skip ahead, but I want to set the record straight. The money I earned in business was substantial. How substantial? Many years later, when my daughters burst on the scene, people thought of us as the poor black family from the ghetto rising up against the white tide of tennis and America. The truth was I had created a company before they were born called Richard Williams Tennis Associates, which I still own, and had saved $810,000, which was all in the bank. I paid my own kids' way through tennis. I didn't want anyone to help me. I could have gotten sponsors, but Venus and Serena were my children, so it was my responsibility to pay for them. I never had to take one penny from anyone.

However, I am getting way ahead of myself. At that time, there were no girls, no wife, and no seventy-five- and seventy-eight-page documented plans, long gone now, that detailed every step of how I was going to raise tennis champions. This was because an important event had yet to occur, one that would change my life and my dreams forever.

I was about to fall in love.

I didn't know a single thing about tennis, and in fact, didn't like it much at all, when I met my future wife, Oracene Price, in the summer of 1978, sitting at a bus stop in Lynwood, California. I believe I fell in love with her the very first moment I saw her. It was one of those once-in-a-lifetime romantic flashes where you see a girl who just knocks you out. That was Oracene for me. It was Sunday afternoon, and a friend of mine, Robert Jackson, and I had just finished playing basketball and were driving home. Oracene was sitting on a bench on the sidewalk, waiting for a bus as we passed. She turned my head right around. She looked so sweet and pretty, I knew I had to find a way to meet her. I just couldn't let her disappear.

I said quickly, "Robert, did you see that girl sitting back there?"

"Yes, I did," he said admiringly.

"I couldn't take my eyes off her. She's so fine. She got those skinny legs and big ole hips. Stop the car and you go talk to her, man. Then you can introduce me."

He shook his head. "Man, she wouldn't talk to no one like me. Why don't *you* go talk to her?"

"I can't," I said. "I'm dating Stacy." I was always honest with women. If I was dating one, I never two-timed her.

He looked at me like I was nuts. "Man, go talk to her. It's just talking, right?"

He drove around the block and we parked, and I went over. My heart was actually beating hard and my usual confidence was all at risk if she didn't respond.

"Excuse me," I said. "My name is Richard Williams."

She ignored me. I said it again. She kept ignoring me and I was afraid the bus would come and Oracene would get on it and go, but finally she loosened up enough to tell me she was from Saginaw, Michigan, and worked as a nurse here in LA. I was impressed that she had been to school, signaling ambition, a quality sorely lacking in so many of the women I met. She was staying in Lynwood, at the home of a girlfriend named Sandra. That was all I could get out of her. Now, it was getting late and she was heading home. She didn't want to talk more to me or tell me anything else. I was desperate. I offered her a lift but she declined. Unwilling to let her go, as she got on the bus, I got back into Robert's car, and followed her all the way to Sandra's house.

It was one of those hot, dry LA afternoons when even the wind was full of scent and promise. I knew I was acting crazy but my head was buzzing. I have always been a romantic man and that day my heart was in control. I parked outside Sandra's house, and got to talk to Oracene a little more. I even got to meet Sandra, who rushed out of the house when she saw Oracene talking to a stranger. I don't think Sandra liked me one bit, but when Oracene went inside, I tried convincing Sandra I was okay.

"You know your friend who's staying here is a fine girl," I said.

She arched an eyebrow. "Oh, yeah?"

"Can you tell me more about her?"

"Nope, she don't want nothin' to do with ya. She say you crazy."

As a last resort, I reached into my pocket and pulled out a hundred-dollar bill. "Listen, Sandra, you can have this if you tell me more about her."

Her jaw dropped. She pushed it away, but I insisted. It bought me the right to sit on her porch and ask lots more questions. Sandra told me how smart Oracene was, and how honest and principled. I learned that Oracene was in her late twenties, and had three young daughters, Yetunde, Isha, and Lyndrea. She also told me Oracene was raising her kids alone. I was terribly impressed she hadn't sunk into bad ways like so many women I knew who were single mothers. She was working hard and taking good care of her girls.

The more Sandra told me about Oracene, the more I knew

I had to see her again. That night, I went to Stacy, the girl I was dating, and told her I wouldn't be seeing her anymore because I had met someone else. Of course, she accused me of having been with Oracene, but I stopped her cold. "I have not been with her," I told her. "Matter of fact, she don't want me at all. I want *her*. Look, wherever your heart is, that's where your desire is. And whatever you desire, if you don't get it, you're not gonna be happy. So to keep from two-timing you, I'm just gonna be honest with you and go take my chances with her."

And that's what I did. I went back to see Oracene the next day and tried my best to soften her up, to get her to like me. I was happy being with her from the first moment I saw her. I spoke to her in a way I had never spoken to anyone before. We spent all our time talking and it was wonderful. I told her what kind of person I was, what kind of home I came from. I told her about all the abuse from white people I'd been through throughout my life, and all the lying and cheating I had done. I told her I had a son named Richard, by a lady named Betty Johnson. I explained I had left Betty because of the presence of gambling and alcohol, but I was doing all I could to take care of my son, and wanted to bring Richard up the right way.

Oracene listened. We grew closer. She liked to cook and actually made food and baked things for me. I took her to the beach and the park and we had picnics. I didn't try to grab her or kiss her. I wouldn't do any of those things. We just talked every minute we were together. I never knew how great it was to be able to be with someone like that. I told her what I wanted to do with my future, and all my plans, and how my business was going, and she told me about what she wanted in life, how important her girls were to her, and how fast they were growing up. We even took a trip to Michigan together so I could meet her parents. I brought them gifts. I liked them as soon as we met, and felt a strong bond with her father. He told me I was in for it because Oracene was so stubborn.

I said jokingly, "If I don't get her to change, I'll bring her back home."

He said, "Son, then you better not take her with you, 'cause she's not gonna change one bit."

I loved Oracene deeply, and as soon as I met her girls, I loved them, too. They were cute and bright and a joy to be with. Soon, things progressed to where Oracene and I made plans to get married. The engagement ring cost me about twelve hundred dollars. I loved how logical Oracene was about a wedding. Unlike most women, she wasn't interested in inviting a million people to a huge party or having a big ceremony, so we decided against a church wedding. When it came time to wed, we had a private marriage ceremony in Long Beach.

One of my best memories in this life was when the preacher said, "Now you can kiss the bride." I swear it was the best kiss I'd ever had in my entire life. I'd kissed Oracene a hundred times before, but on that particular day, when I kissed her, it was the best kiss I ever had and I still remember it that way to this day.

As a ready-made family of five, we needed a bigger place to live, so I bought us a house in Long Beach, a few blocks from the beach. After the wedding, Oracene, Yetunde, Isha, and Lyndrea, and I all moved in together. It was a good house and we could all walk to the beach together. We loved it.

I have to admit, even I was surprised at the suddenness of it all. In one fell swoop, I was now a family man. I was married, with three daughters. As a child, I had lived with my mother and three sisters. Here I was again, living in a house filled with four women—and I loved it. I loved being a father and taking care of the girls, whom I loved as my own. My mother had been very firm when I told her I was moving in with Oracene and her children. She said, "Don't do it unless you can love those children like your very own." I did love them. It was easy. They were great kids, smart and loving, and we had great relationships.

Yetunde was the oldest, around seven years old, then Isha, around five, and Lyn, who was one. They were such great people. I used to take them to school and to museums and parks to see different shows. I used to talk to them about politics and the world and about law. I used to say that any black person who didn't know the law was at a disadvantage. Maybe it started Isha on the track to becoming a lawyer.

I think it's important your kids think you can do things no one else can do. You earn their respect. One time I told Isha to cut the grass. We didn't have a lawn mower, so she told me she couldn't cut it.

I said, "Okay, get me a pair of scissors and I'll cut it."

"It can't be done that way," she insisted.

"It sure can," I said, and took a pair of scissors and cut every inch of grass with them while Isha watched in surprise.

It's all in the teaching. You can make kids think they are weak or you can make them think they are strong. Your strength is no more than an attitude you have about yourself. If you believe you can't do something, you can't do it. The minute you believe you can, you can. This is a can-do world. It's not a can't-do world.

Some years ago, Isha asked me if I remembered cutting the grass with the scissors.

I said, "Sure, I remember."

She said, "At the time I didn't think it could be done but you did, so I wanted to do it, too. You know, later on, I did?"

I knew. I had seen her duplicate my effort with these same scissors. That's the way I tried to bring them up. There was nothing on this earth they could not do. I taught belief in yourself. If you don't believe in yourself, no one else will. People see your attitude about success or failure even before they shake your hand. They see if you look them straight in the eye. They watch how you hold your head.

I remembered my family in Shreveport, unable to envision a world filled with possibilities or promise. I didn't understand it then, but I understood it now. When you condition people to inequality instead of equality, injustice instead of justice, failure instead of success, and hate instead of love, it is almost impossible for them to escape deep feelings of self-doubt and mistrust.

Was I a victim of that, too?

I had come a long way since Shreveport. I owned my own business and made money, but real wealth, fame, and power, the three components of my American dream, seemed not within my grasp. Reluctant to accept that idea, I propelled my thoughts to an elevated state. I would not live a contained, restricted, or limited life. I would think out of the box. I was imaginative and creative and I was adamant about navigating my own course. Every man has to make his own footprints in the sand. I was the navigator of my own destiny. Despite being ridiculed for being different, my desire to transcend the world's expectations would not falter.

Our house was located near the ocean and was my place of refuge when I wanted to think. What I loved most was the smell of the sea breeze at night. Many evenings I strolled along the shore with my thoughts as unfettered as the wind. I loved sitting in the family room, which was also my office. My large desk sat in the middle of the floor, dominating the room. I decorated the corners with large green plants with leaves that looked like outstretched arms. The television sat against the wall adjacent to a large sofa, and a large mirror reflected a beam of light that shone through the small crack in the curtains.

This was the room where it all started.

One Sunday, we were all watching television and I asked Yetunde to change the channels. We didn't have a remote, so she patiently turned from one channel to the next and waited for my approval. As programs flashed across the screen, something caught my attention, but she had already turned to another channel. I hopped out of my chair and quickly turned it back. It was a tennis match. Actually, the match was over. I will never forget standing there in amazement, watching the tournament director present a twenty-five-year-old professional tennis player from Romania named Virginia Ruzici a forty-thousand-dollar check for winning the tournament.

Announcer Bud Collins's next words rang in my ears. "That's not bad for four days' work."

I didn't think it was possible for anyone to make that kind of money in four days, especially a woman. I couldn't get it out of my mind. In a couple of days? Really? The very next morning I went to the store and bought a newspaper. I pored through it eagerly and found the tennis results. My interest was confirmed when I saw an article about Ruzici's victory and the prize money.

Without hesitation, I said to myself, "I'm going to have two kids and put them in tennis."

I raced home and went into my office and read the article over and over again. I found myself fantasizing about my as-yet-unborn daughters playing tennis. If one woman could win that much money, I wanted *two* daughters to play the game. Double the winnings! After that, I sat in my office thinking and planning everything I'd have to do to succeed. The more I thought about it, the more realistic the idea became.

Yet, with any new venture, there is always the insistent insidious voice of skepticism.

I don't know a thing about tennis.

How am I going to teach them a game I can't even play?

What if my wife doesn't want to have more children?

Why do I always think of these crazy ideas?

Feelings of doubt rocked me, but I had always been a dreamer, obsessed with originality, so why was this any different? Whenever I had a major decision to make I used to look into the night sky for a sign or some confirmation to reassure me. That night I went outside, lay in the backyard, and gazed at the stars the way I used to when I was a boy. I remembered Chili Bowl and me lying like that in the yard with our hands behind our heads, gazing into the sky with twigs hanging from our mouths, talking about all the things we wanted to do when we grew up. I knew what he would have said to me about my plan. "You can do it, Richard!"

I just wished he had been there to say it.

A big bright star sat apart from the rest. I thought, *My children will be set apart from the rest of the tennis players just like that star. They won't be set apart because they're African Americans, either. They will be distinguished because they are going to dominate the game.*

I fell asleep on the ground and dreamed I had two daughters. I was unable to see their faces but they called me Daddy. Their voices were angelic and sweet and slowly faded into the distance as I woke up. Several raindrops touched my face but I could still hear the sound of their voices.

"I'm going to have two daughters," I sang as I went inside from the rain. I could feel it in my soul.

I always believed in planning ahead. My motto was, "When you fail to plan, you plan to fail." I went into my office and began to plan for the day my daughters would dominate tennis. My first plan was a seventy-eight-page typewritten document covering every aspect of tennis training for my daughters. Forgetting the most obvious problem of not having any daughters, my most serious issue was that the game of tennis had never interested me. I thought it was a sissy sport. It lacked the masculine strength and tenacity I admired in basketball, football, and even golf. Hitting a little ball with a big racquet seemed feminine. In addition, it wasn't popular among black people, at least the ones I knew. Yet, in a funny way, that made it an open field. What were the reasons black people shied away from tennis? Could I turn that to our advantage? Had any of the great African-American athletes dissected the game the way they had basketball or baseball? Was there anything to learn from Gibson, Ashe, or others? Would the entrance of strong, fast, ghetto-bred black people into the game change it as dramatically as it had all other sports?

Despite my dislike of the game, I grew even more convinced it was perfect for my future daughters. My plan was simple: to bring two children out of the ghetto to the forefront of a white-dominated game. Could it be done? I hoped so. In fact, I was beyond hope. I was certain. It was just a matter of time. Eliminating the last doubts from my mind, I wrote a final seventy-five-page tennis-training plan for myself, Oracene, and my daughters-to-be, detailing every step of the road we would travel, more than two and a half years before they were both born.

I was now short only one thing. Daughters. Happily, however, affection was always something Oracene and I shared. Also, Oracene herself had been an athlete as a kid, playing sports with her brothers. She understood my plan. Equally important, she understood my desire to have children of our own. She agreed gladly, and work on that part of the project began almost immediately.

I still had a lot to learn. I had never played tennis. I didn't even know how to keep score. Clearly, I was at a disadvantage. Besides, given the confrontations with white people I had had throughout my life, how could I get involved in this sport? Would I have to go through the back door? Would I have to beg and plead? Would I have to say "Yes, sir" and "No, sir"? Would my family and I be treated with equality or inequality?

After investigating the cost of racquets and balls, I went to Paramount Sports in Hollywood, California, and spoke with owners Bill and Ted Hodges, whom I knew pretty well. They were brothers and tennis enthusiasts. When I told them what I was planning to do, they laughed.

"You're planning a tennis career for children who aren't even born yet?" Ted asked with a look of disbelief on his face. "Richard, I always thought you were a little off the wall," he joked. "But this?"

"You're laughing now," I said. "But one day you'll look back and remember this day and know I wasn't kidding."

"Do you even know how to play tennis, Richard?" Bill asked between chuckles.

"Not today, but I will as soon as you sell me some balls."

Bill and Ted sold used balls. Most had been used during a match or at a tennis club, and only cost a dime. I bought three hundred. I also bought a video instruction tape and a tennis book.

"How are you going to play tennis without a racquet?" Ted asked.

"I have a racquet," I boasted as I pushed my basket out the door. "I found a really good one at the Goodwill."

Ted's laugh echoed behind me. "Learning to play tennis from a book, using a secondhand racquet and old balls? Now I've seen it all."

I always learned by looking and listening. It was how I knew the distance I needed to run to escape the murderous pursuers of my youth, or how to make bids to run my company. I went to a park off Compton Avenue, in the Watts section of LA, close to where I lived. I wasn't sure how to get a game, or even find someone to hit with, but as I walked around the courts, I saw a trim, older black man hitting balls to a strong young male player and instructing him as he did. I was impressed. They hit so fast it sounded like gunfire.

I stood there watching, my racquet dangling from my hand. After about fifteen minutes, the old man yelled to me, "Don't just stand there and watch, son. You won't learn to hit the ball that way. When he gets tired, you can hop right in."

It was a good chance to see what I had learned, so as soon as the other player left, I got on the court and tried to put into practice what I had seen in my tennis books and tapes.

It was a disaster.

"Look at the ball and stop trying to hit it so doggone hard," my teacher yelled as I blasted another into the fence.

We hit for about fifteen minutes and, as I was picking up balls, he called me over.

"May I speak to you a minute, young man?"

"Yes, sir?"

"My name is Oliver and I give tennis lessons out here every day except Sunday. That's my day off," he explained as the wind carried his alcohol-sodden breath to me. "You look like you need a few lessons, son. What's your name?"

"My name is Richard Williams," I replied. "I would be hon-
ored to come out and take some lessons with you, Mr. Oliver.
How much do you charge?"

"Hmmm." He sighed and rubbed a wrinkled hand across
his rough gray-bearded chin. "My prices are very economical,
very affordable. Just bring me a pint of whiskey every time you
have a lesson and we'll be all right." He smiled. "I'm out here
at eight o'clock in the morning and I hit until lunchtime. I
takes me a little break and I'm usually back on the court by one
o'clock and I stay here until about six-thirty or so. It depends
on how much whiskey I get. The more I get, the longer I stay.
That's my policy," he said, and laughed.

"I'll see you tomorrow at five o'clock," I said, and walked
away with a smile on my face, too.

Oliver's nickname was Old Whiskey, and it was well-known
he drank for breakfast, lunch, and dinner, yet somehow kept
his composure long enough to give tennis lessons. At first,
I was just happy not to pay the fifty to one hundred dollars
many other pros were charging. Soon, I fell in love with Old
Whiskey. He was an unbelievable human being. It turned out
he had actually done some work with Arthur Ashe and with
Jimmy Connors. I didn't know much about either, but the
minute you started studying the game you learned those two
names right away.

The next day, I took my second official tennis lesson. It
was another disaster. I sprayed balls all over the place. I ran
around like a fool. I missed ball after ball, as if my racquet had
no strings in it.

Whenever I missed a shot, Oliver would yell, "Richard,
you're hitting like old whiskey."

During one lesson, Oliver reached down to get a ball and
his bottle of whiskey fell and broke. He walked off the court

and sat down on a bench. I went over and sat next to him. I said nothing, just reached inside my pocket and took out a ten-dollar bill, put it in his hand, and closed my hand over his.

He nodded gratefully and we sat for a while.

"Richard," he said quietly, "I've worked with a lot of young people, and a lot of my kids went on to college. Most of 'em graduated and they still come back and see me every now and then. I feel so proud when one of my kids makes it through. I worked with two players from UCLA. One of the boys was white and the other one was black. Both of them turned pro and ranked pretty decent on the tour."

"That's great," I said.

"You know what's sad about it?"

"What?" I asked curiously.

"I expected the black boy to come back and see me, but he never did, not one time after he turned professional. When he was interviewed, he never so much as mentioned my name. Don't get me wrong. It's not like I was looking for him to give me credit or anything. I just thought he would be proud to say he learned the game from an old black man in the ghetto."

"That would have been nice," I agreed.

"He played a tournament here one time and I bought myself a ticket and went to see him play. I stood out there waiting for him after the game with all the other fans and he walked right past me. He looked me directly in the eyes and kept going. He didn't speak or anything. He was so serious-looking. The funny thing about it is the white boy came back to see me several times. Once, he came out and we hit some balls for old times' sake. That's amazing, ain't it? I guess people's just people," he said with surprising gentleness in his voice.

Time blew by, and soon I had only one lesson left with Oliver. When I missed a ball, he yelled, "You're still hitting the ball like old whiskey."

Afterward, Oliver and I sat on the bench and I listened to him talk for the last time. He looked me up and down. "You have great feet, Richard. I like the way you line your feet up behind the ball. That's the smart way to do it. Most of the people I work with have messed-up feet and that's why their games can't get no better. If you got bad feet, you got bad technique. I heard you learning how to play tennis so you can teach your children, but they ain't even been born yet. Man, Richard, you are something. I hope I live long enough to see your children make it."

I said, "I think they gonna make it, too."

"Well, every now and then God sends somebody to show the world that anything and everything is possible with Him. You believe in God, Richard?"

I nodded. "I was raised in the Church of Christ and my mama was a prayer warrior. She used to tell me God had a job for me to do." I laughed. "I sure hope this is the job because I'm definitely gonna need Him on my side for it."

Oliver stared toward the sky for a moment and said, "God is always gonna be on your side. Just keep your eye on the prize."

I thanked him, and packed, and stood up to go.

With a smile on his unshaven face, Oliver stood, grabbed my hand, and said, "Come back and see me sometime, Richard, but don't make no promises you can't keep."

That was it. He let my hand go, went back to the court, and started hitting balls with his next lesson. The funny thing was that I disagreed with almost everything Old Whiskey taught me. I disagreed with the footwork because I had a basic conflict with the closed stance all the pros taught, but I had not yet perfected the open stance and the power and speed it would bring to women's tennis. But he had started me, and believed in me, and helped me reach a better level.

Sadly, Mr. Oliver died a few years later, long before he could see the things he taught me blossom in my daughters. Still, I remember him fondly and, to this day, I hope he knew how much he gave me.

CHAPTER **SIXTEEN**

From that time on, tennis consumed me. It was a good thing I could manage my security company from home at night, and had flexible hours during the day, because I spent every other waking hour learning the game. I bought more books and magazines. My thirst for knowledge evolved into a tennis video collection and a library of books. All the reading and studying I did generated more questions, so I spoke with individuals from the National Junior Tennis League (NJTL) and the United States Tennis Association (USTA). A lot of the information I acquired made sense, but the major question I still had was the proper way the feet should go.

Everyone I spoke to agreed that the closed stance should be used on both the backhand and forehand sides.

"How can you hit a ball north when your body isn't turned that way?" I asked.

The consensus was, "This is the way it's supposed to be, and the way it will always be."

Maybe it was supposed to be that way for them, but I thought I had a better way. They were all climbing the same hill, the same way. I decided to climb my own hill. I decided the way to go was an *open* stance.

I went to the park and hit ball after ball against the wall every day for a month trying to perfect my footwork. Consistency was the name of the game. The ball's speed off the wall forced me to get my racquet back early and to hit under the ball. During my self-instruction, I also worked on getting my elbow up on every shot with a long follow-through. I also substituted a quick sideways hop and jump on the baseline that let me get wider faster and return sharp-angled shots down the line, for the side-to-side spider-steps most instructors taught.

After a month of practice, I got back on the court. I put on a pair of cutoff jeans, a faded, wrinkled T-shirt, and a pair of dirty tennis shoes without socks. If this attire was proper for a pickup game of basketball, it had to be okay for the far less physical game of tennis. After inspecting myself in the mirror, I sprayed some sheen on my Jheri curl and patted it down. Not one string of hair on my head was out of place. Quite pleased with myself, I grabbed my racquet and some balls and headed out.

Whenever I drove through the city people stared at me, thanks to my 1975 Oldsmobile. The defective muffler was so loud it sounded like a tank, the headliner sagged in the middle of the roof, and the lights and the air conditioner had minds of their own—sometimes they worked and other times they didn't. I drove through the black ghetto neighborhoods of Watts, Compton, and Long Beach, looking for tennis courts. I wanted to locate them so I knew exactly where to take my future daughters when I started training them. There were at least three or four tennis courts in every area I visited, and I made notes on all of them. I decided to try my skills on the courts in Lynwood, a black ghetto area in South LA. To my surprise, when I pulled into the parking lot, it looked like I was at a country club. There was an old Jaguar, an aging Porsche, a Mercedes convertible, a Corvette, a Mustang, and four Cadillacs—one Coupe de Ville, two Eldorados, and a Fleetwood.

Lynwood Park, being where it was, drew black players, and was sad proof that most black people in the ghetto had better cars than they had houses. I half expected an attendant to run out and offer to valet park my car. I grabbed my racquet and balls and walked to the fence enclosing the courts. For a long time, I just watched and listened to the players. They were the best-dressed group of black people I had ever seen. The men had their shirts tucked inside their shorts and the women wore extremely short skirts. Their tennis shoes were so clean they looked unused. All wore headbands and wristbands; some men wore gold chains. One man sprayed sheen on his Jheri curl hair, picked it out, and patted it before he went onto the court. The women constantly touched up their heavy makeup and reapplied fresh lipstick. I couldn't help thinking that no matter how they dressed, none of them would be permitted into any of Los Angeles's country clubs unless they were looking for a cleaning person or a caddy.

It didn't take long to see they had everything except game. Most of them couldn't play a lick. Evidently, appearance was the shot of the day.

"Brother, why are you standing outside the fence?" a man asked me, interrupting my thoughts.

"I'm just looking," I replied.

"You can come in," he said, and pushed open the gate. As soon as I walked onto the court, everyone stopped. I mean, they literally stopped playing and stared at me for a moment and then burst into laughter.

"Hey, man, my name is Professor," my guide said and reached for my hand and shook it. "And this is Colonel," he introduced the annoyed-looking man next to him.

"My name is Richard Williams and I was just looking for a place where I can come hit," I explained.

"Can you play?" Colonel asked flatly. "'Cause we take our tennis very serious, man. We don't like no rookies on the court."

"I'm probably not as good as you guys, but I hit the ball pretty decent."

"How long have you been playing?" Colonel asked.

"I picked up a racquet for the first time two months ago. I haven't been playing long but I'm really beginning to understand the game," I replied.

Colonel walked away without another word, pulling Professor with him, but I could still hear their conversation.

"Professor, I hope he don't think he's going to play on these courts. Two months? What can you learn in two lousy months?" Colonel said in a belligerent tone.

"Shush, Colonel." Professor put his finger to his mouth. "Look at it this way. We'll have someone we can beat up on all the time."

I stood listening to these pretentious assholes talking about me like I was invisible. As far as I was concerned, just dressing like a tennis player didn't make you one.

Professor and Colonel came back over. Colonel said, "I think we'll let you play on this court."

I snapped, "You must be confused, because I wasn't asking for permission."

I walked outside the fence and watched. They had prehistoric strokes, horrible footwork, and no strategy. But they were so high-class that after they played a set, they changed balls and tossed the old ones into the garbage. When they came off the court and gathered in the parking lot to laugh, talk, and brag, I went and took the balls out of the garbage. Everyone looked at me. One of the women asked in a high-pitched voice, "What is he doing? Why is he taking those balls out of the garbage can?"

Someone replied, "He can't afford tennis clothes, so you know he can't afford balls. As long as he's out here we don't need a trash man."

I walked past the group to my car. Before getting in, I called back, "I'll see you tomorrow."

The next day, I got a chance to play. The rule was you had to bring your own balls. I brought my ten-cent used ones. When I took them out of my plastic bag, Colonel yelled, "I'm not playing with those old balls, man. If you don't have new balls, you can't play."

I didn't say a word. I just stood on my side of the court holding my racquet in one hand and three old balls in the other.

"Let me know when you're ready," I said.

After a few minutes, Colonel said, "Okay, hit the damn ball, man. This is ridiculous. I don't know why they let you out here in the first place."

We hit back and forth. During the warm-up, I didn't get a chance to hit many balls back because he kept hitting them hard or away from me. While he was hitting like a mad dog,

I studied his strokes and footwork. In the middle of hitting, I asked, "Why do you hit the ball with a closed stance?"

At first, he didn't answer. I asked again. "Why do you hit the ball with a closed stance?"

"I heard you the first time. That's the way you're supposed to hit it. If you were a real tennis player, you would know that. Besides, it doesn't matter how I hit the ball. I can beat your ass."

We took some practice serves and I noticed he had a few problems, so I asked him, "Why do you stop the flow of motion when you serve the ball, and why do you toss the ball so high and then let it drop too low before you hit it? You'll never have a good serve that way."

Colonel deliberately served a flat ball over the net so fast I didn't see it coming. "Don't worry about my serve. You just worry about trying to return the fire." He laughed.

We played, and I lost 6–0, 6–0.

Colonel rejoiced like he had just beat Arthur Ashe or Jimmy Connors. I didn't care. I was more interested in how my footwork should change to make the proper distance to the ball and not run into it or past it.

Colonel explained, "It won't make a difference, 'cause you can't beat me no way."

I continued to come to the courts to play. No one was happy about my being there but they were happy to play me. I lost to everyone, even the women. After three months of losing, I bought a big-faced racquet and hoped it would help. One day, I played a woman named Jo-Jo, and she hit the ball so hard I missed it.

Jo-Jo asked, "How could you miss the ball with that big old racquet? That's ridiculous."

"I was working on my open stance."

She snorted. "That's why you lose all the time, because you keep trying all that junk."

She wasn't wrong. I lost all the time. Still, considering I only had my lessons with Oliver and my work on the backboard, I didn't think my losses were that bad. The guys at the park didn't agree with me. I lost so much, they made up a song.

Someone's got to win, someone's got to lose.
Richard keeps losing 'cause he's an open-stance fool.

I was also known for bringing my water in an old plastic gallon milk jug and never bringing a towel. I saw no need for a towel because I didn't sweat like the rest of them. When they played me, they did all the running. I usually stood in one spot and worked on one part of my game. A lot of hostility built up between us. It got even worse when they found out I was learning the game to teach my children who hadn't been born yet. One evening, after they gathered in the parking lot, they started teasing me about my dream.

"Richard," mocked Top Spin, "you really think you're going to have tennis champions? Man, that's a fool's dream. I can count the blacks who made it in tennis on one hand. What makes you think your children will be good enough?"

Colonel, who took every opportunity to insult me, added, "The way you play, you couldn't teach your kids nothing. If you did, they would get beat up on just like you."

It was then that a man named Nathaniel cleared his throat and said sternly, "All of you guys laugh at Richard. You should go home and do the same thing." He kept on, angrily. "Tell me what black man you know plans for his children's future before they are born. Most black men just make a bunch of babies and don't take care of them. Richard is willing to sacrifice himself for his family. All of you are just a selfish bunch of niggers."

The comments and jokes had only one effect on me. I was more determined than ever to improve my game. I would make believers out of everyone who said the open stance had no place in tennis. I stopped going to the tennis courts and began to practice again. Every Monday, Tuesday, and Wednesday morning before work, I hit three hundred forehands down the line with an open stance. On my lunch break, I hit hundreds of forehands crosscourt. When I got off work I hit three hundred backhands down the line and then crosscourt, all with an open stance. I hired kids to pick up balls so I didn't have to slow down. On Thursdays, Fridays, and Saturdays, I worked on my serves and volleys. If it rained, I practiced in a gym with a secondhand Lobster ball machine I bought. Hitting off the waxed hardwood floors was difficult but it taught me a valuable lesson—how to get my racquet back faster than anyone who played the game. Once I learned to control both forehand and backhand, it would be difficult to beat me.

I also played basketball and baseball because these sports helped me see the ball early, and throwing the ball helped with my serve. Later, I would have Venus and Serena throw a football to strengthen those same muscles. I also believed balance was an important and underemphasized part of the game. To enhance my balance, I took dance lessons. At my first lesson, the teacher asked me to face her so we could dance. I put my left side to her front, the way you turn your body to hit a tennis ball.

"What are you doing?" she asked.

"Getting ready to dance," I replied.

She shook her head. "No, no, no! You can't dance that way."

"Well that's the way people hit a tennis ball," I replied.

She sighed. "I don't know anything about tennis balls, but I do know you can't dance with me if your side is facing me. It doesn't make sense. Let's try again."

I turned my right side to her this time.

She said, "You're doing the same thing. It's just a different side. What are you trying to do?"

I replied, "That's the way they do it on the tennis court."

"Mr. Williams, I have never held a tennis racquet in my hand and I know absolutely nothing about the game but I do know if you hit a ball that way you won't have any balance, and if you have to run to the other side, you'll have a problem. To play any sport you have to have good balance and great feet."

I explained, "I'm planning to teach my daughters tennis and I want to make sure I understand how to shift my body from side to side, how to make explosive moves and keep my balance. Do you think you can help me with that?" I asked.

"Do you have pictures or a video I can study to see how you hit the tennis ball?" she asked.

"Yes, I have something in the car. I'll be right back."

I rushed to the car and brought back a video. She took the video out of my hand and inserted it in the VCR. We watched the tape and she made several notes. When the tape stopped, she nodded.

"Now I understand what you were doing when you turned to the side to dance with me. Everyone in the tape hits the ball that way. I'm surprised they don't fall on their faces. I think if you want to hit forward, you should face forward. The people in the tape face to the side. I saw something else on the tape, too. When they ran wide to get the ball, they were unable to recover because they couldn't shift their weight. On some of the shots, I think the hitter should have taken a bigger first step."

"I agree. I've seen that, too."

"Would you like me to incorporate all of those things into a dance sequence for you?" she asked.

"Yes, I would. I really would appreciate it," I replied.

"I'm going to include some special stretching exercises to make sure your muscles don't tighten up. That will help your flexibility."

I smiled. That was music to my ears.

"Okay, then. I can meet with you one night a week in the evening but a lot of it will involve practicing on your own. What night do you want your lesson? By the way, my fee is fifteen dollars a week."

"Wednesday night," I told her, and I took my first lesson that night, and took one every Wednesday thereafter for almost a year.

I have always believed that you can't know if a theory is correct until you test it. That idea served me well when the Klan boys came for me and I learned how far I really needed to run to escape. It served me well in Chicago when I beat the cops who nearly killed me; and in Los Angeles, it helped me figure out how to get around Buddy and go into business for myself. An untested theory is like raw meat—you can't tell how it tastes till it's cooked.

After three months of rigid practice, cross-training, and dancing, I was ready and eager to return to the tennis courts.

I had my theories.

Now it was time to test them.

CHAPTER **SEVENTEEN**

When I drove back into the parking lot at Lynwood Park, very little had changed. Professor and Colonel were playing doubles, and by the celebratory look on their faces, they were winning. Lola and Nathaniel played mixed doubles against Tina and Rudy, and more than once Lola's high-pitched voice filled the air.

"That ball wasn't out. Show me the mark, Rudy. You just show me the mark!"

In the months I had been gone, there were a few new faces, and with them, new attitudes. Truck was a tall brother who, at six-foot-eight, looked more like a basketball player than a tennis player. He covered the court extremely well, and his long wingspan and surprisingly quick feet made him difficult to beat. He played an aggressive serve-and-volley game and closed the point without concern for his opponent's safety. He'd take your head off with the ball if you came to the net.

Omar was a college-educated brother who had fought in Vietnam. Since his return from the war, he had changed his name and become a vegetarian and an advocate for black issues. He was articulate, intelligent, and never backed down from a confrontation. It was no secret the group disliked me, but I honestly believe they despised Omar.

Omar played in a dashiki instead of a regular shirt. Unlike most black men, who had Jheri curls, he had shoulder-length dreadlocks like woven rope. He lived in an old green army step-van with a picture of Africa painted on one side, and two black fists with the caption "Black Power" on the other. Inside, bookcases were filled with volumes on Africa, black history, slavery, segregation, poverty, education, sociology, and war. He had a television that ran on batteries, a small refrigerator, and a file cabinet. A sheet of psychedelic-painted plywood served as a desk, with a framed copy of his college degree on it. Up front, the driver's area was carpeted and the seats were covered in black fur.

The veteran's disability check from the government was Omar's primary source of income. To earn additional money, he gave lectures at radical white college students' meetings. Omar's message was clear. He preached blacks should go back to Africa. The motherland was the only way we would ever truly know who we were as a people. He also claimed the reason blacks suffered from high blood pressure, diabetes, and other illnesses was the food we ate.

"The food we eat is traced back to slavery. The master got choice meat, we got the throwaway. If he killed a pig, he got delicious pork chops. We got the pig's guts or intestine (chitterlings), his tail, feet, and lips. If he killed a chicken, he feasted on the savory meat, we got the feet, neck, liver, and gizzards. We always got the scraps from the master's table and from then until now we're still eating scrap."

He also believed blacks would always be oppressed and live in poverty and terrible neighborhoods if they didn't understand the power of a dollar.

"Black people spend a lot of money in this country buying everything, but we don't own anything. Look at all these people dressed up in those expensive tennis clothes. Where did they buy them? I'm willing to bet they left our community and took their dollars to the white man's store. The black man used to own stores but now every other nationality is moving in and taking our money. Are we blind or are we just plain crazy?"

Whenever Omar talked that way, the group thought he was insulting them personally. It was interesting to me. As the years had rolled on, my ideas were no longer considered so crazy. More people were speaking the way I spoke and beginning to illuminate the real nature of the black race's problems in white America.

On my first day back, I didn't play. I just watched. When I pulled into the parking lot the next day, Colonel came up to me.

"Richard, I saw you hanging outside the fence yesterday. I bet you were scared to come in because you thought you had to play me."

I got out of my car, grabbed a racquet and balls, and headed for the court. Colonel walked behind me and kept taunting, "Look, everybody, Richard's back. Let's give him a round of applause."

Everyone started clapping and laughing.

Colonel continued in a loud voice, "A lot of things have

changed since you left. Do you want to play me, Richard?" he asked smugly.

"Not today," I replied and went to hit against the backboard.

"See there, everybody? He's too scared to play."

I was ready to play and I knew I would win, but I didn't accept a single game. I hit against the backboard and watched. Meanwhile, Colonel took every opportunity to agitate me and got upset when it didn't work. By the third week, however, I'd had enough. I walked onto the court and yelled over to the Colonel, "I'm ready when you are."

Colonel grabbed his racquet, tennis bag, and water jug, and walked onto the court. Everyone stopped playing and came to watch. We hit a few groundstrokes and I purposely hit every other ball into the net or out. Then I came in on a few shots and worked on my volleys.

"Are you ready yet?" he asked.

"No, I want to hit a few serves and overheads."

"Take all the time you need. It won't make a difference because you're going to lose."

After we warmed up, he took out a coin. "Heads or tails?"

"You serve," I replied, and went to the baseline.

Colonel's first serve was an ace. He started pumping his fist and saying, "Yes." His second and third serves were aces, too. At 40–Love, he served the ball to my forehand and I hit a crosscourt winner.

"Lucky shot!" he yelled.

At 40–15, he served and I hit a backhand winner down the line.

At 40–30, he served wide and I nailed it down the line. He just stood and stared.

It was deuce, and he served. I stepped into the ball and hit a crosscourt winner. At ad in, my return of serve was a drop shot that forced him to run in. He got to the ball but floated it back. I was already at the net so I volleyed the ball past him and won the game.

He was unable to handle my kick serve, so I held every service in the first set. My drop shots, lobs, slice, and angles proved too much for him. I won the first set 6–0. He was very quiet. I jumped up 5–0 so fast in the second set, he looked like he wanted to throw his racquet at me.

I served for the match.

After the third serve, I was up 40–0. Game, set, and match point. Colonel looked very serious. I served down the T and he couldn't get his racquet anywhere near the ball. It was an ace, and the match. I had beaten the loudmouthed Colonel 6–0, 6–0.

Someone started to sing the song they wrote about me, but with different words.

Someone got to win, someone's got to lose . . .
Colonel come off the court looking like a fool.

I went to the net to shake Colonel's hand but he refused. "I don't want to shake your hand. You think you did something. You just got lucky, that's all."

My game got better and better. Impressed by my ability, the group started to bet on my matches. They brought in players from other areas to play me. I encouraged that because I knew their games so it was no longer a challenge. These courts were my first real training ground and my most consistent regimen. To be ready when the time came to train my daughters, I needed people who played better than I did to raise my game.

To keep enhancing my feet, hand, and eye coordination, I took boxing lessons. The smell of the dusty, cramped room brought back memories of my earlier boxing days in Chicago, memories I wanted to forget. I had trained at a local gym, hoping to turn professional. My reflexes were sharp, my feet were quick, and my hands were fast. For many young Negroes, boxing seemed to present a chance to escape poverty and oppression. For me, as for most, it was a pipe dream.

Boxing demanded commitment, perseverance, stamina, strength, power, control, patience, tolerance, and focus. We were all just kids, foolishly convinced we were going to be the next heavyweight champion of the world. After six months of training, I fought my first fight. To say I was nervous and scared is an understatement. My opponent was three inches taller, outweighed me by forty pounds, and was the meanest-looking man I had ever seen. At the bell, he just walked over to the ropes and push-pulled his body back and forth. I wasn't sure what to do so I waited patiently with my fists in front of my face.

He yelled, "Where did you get young blood from? Why do you keep putting these boys in the ring with me? Y'all know they can't fight, man. Damn! Okay, boy, I'm about to knock you out."

I started bouncing around and moving from side to side to show him I wasn't a chump. I threw a right jab and it lightly brushed against his jaw. I followed with a left jab that missed him completely. He hit me with a right uppercut and the lights went out. I don't remember anything after that. To this day, I have no idea how I got out of the ring. When I woke in the dressing room, my trainer was standing over me. He dropped some money on my chest and said, "Good fight, kid. Better luck next time."

I told myself there wasn't going to be a next time but I found myself back in the ring, still getting the shit beat out of me. One night I got hit so hard, I flew over the rope, fell, and hit my head on a chair. It was enough. I was tired of getting knocked out in the first round.

Boxing was a part of my life I did not want to revisit, but I was a man on a mission. This time around, I wasn't interested in getting in a ring. I was interested in footwork and hand movement. I videotaped various boxers, took the tapes home, and studied them until I mastered the movements. I bought a punching bag, hung it up in the backyard, and practiced.

My height was a bit beyond six feet, and Oracene was a six-footer. I was pretty sure our daughters would be at least as tall. Height was a good feature. If tennis was a washout, they could become basketball players, a sport I loved far more than tennis anyway. But would they be true athletes? Some claimed athleticism was inherited. If that was true, I knew my daughters would be great. Oracene was terrific at sports, and I had always been a successful athlete. As a basketball player, I could shoot, rebound, dribble, and pass with the best of them. In football, I was as fast as the wind, and if anyone tried to tackle me, I blew right past him. My attitude was I could not be stopped—the same mentality I planned to instill in my daughters now that I had game enough to teach them.

I was out to prove that in the upcoming eighties, powder-puff hitters with lots of spin would no longer dominate women's tennis. The game would evolve. Unlike the past, when big people couldn't change direction, stop on a dime, run, or move well, I would introduce a new generation of players: bigger, better, faster, taller.

That was my idea. That was the plan.

My daughters would inherit my knowledge and take the world by storm, as soon as they were born.

CHAPTER **EIGHTEEN**

To my eternal love and gratitude, Venus Ebony Starr Williams arrived in this world on June 17, 1980, and Serena Jameka Williams arrived on September 26, 1981.

I had my game and I had my girls. It was time to put them together. The trouble was, I didn't know that following my plan was about to expose us to the worst side of life, and put our very lives in danger. I really had no idea of the hell to which I was initially consigning my family or the pain I would suffer as a result. What I also did not know was that from here on in, tennis wasn't going to be a game. Not anymore.

Not when you play it in the ghetto.

In the third week of March 1983, I moved my family from Long Beach to Compton in South Central Los Angeles, to a house I bought at 1117 East Stockton Street. It was a terrible change from the tranquility of Long Beach. Compton was lost in a murder spree that would last for twenty years and leave 1,397 people dead from gang- and drug-related violence. It was a world of crime and bloodshed and soon we were trapped in the middle of daily gun battles and shootouts. We quickly learned how to escape the bullets that flew through the air unconcerned about their next victims—we fell to our knees in the posture of prayer and crawled like defenseless children to safety.

There is no real hiding place in a war zone. Gang members controlled the city and put its citizens under martial law. For almost all the senior citizens, it was total lockdown. The gangs preyed on their helpless victims through intimidation, threats, violence, and murder. They ruled the streets of Compton, shooting people without hesitation. Thugs commanded every corner, willing to kill or be killed, just to protect their territory. Life had little meaning. People died just for the hell of it.

What led me to Compton was my belief that the greatest champions came out of the ghetto. I had studied sports successes like Muhammad Ali, and great thinkers like Malcolm X. I saw where they came from. As part of my plan, I decided it was where the girls were going to grow up, too. It would make them tough, give them a fighter's mentality. They'd be used to combat. And how much easier would it be to play in front of thousands of white people if they had already learned to play in front of scores of armed gang members?

Venus was almost three years old and Serena was nearing two. Before Compton, we were living about a block from the beach. It was beautiful. So when the family learned I was moving us, Oracene said, "I'm not gonna move to Compton. There's a limit, Richard!"

I told her she didn't have to move, but I was going, and we could visit each other as often as she liked. In Long Beach, I was paying a huge house note of over one thousand dollars a month. In Compton, the house I bought was twenty-five thousand dollars and the monthly payment was around $135.00. That freed up a lot of money so I could spend less time earning, and more time training the girls. We talked about it a lot and Oracene still didn't want to move, but my mind was made up.

After a while, she decided she would move to Compton and asked me what the house was like. I did not want to tell her the truth. It was a mess.

"You have to see it for yourself," I said.

When Oracene and the older kids saw it for themselves, only Lyn, Venus, and Serena didn't have a problem because they were too young to understand what a drop their lifestyle had taken. Oracene, Yetunde, and Isha balked major league. When Oracene saw people shooting up drugs, and gang members standing on the corner, she refused to stay. She remained in Long Beach while I took the girls with me.

Now I had the type of environment I wanted—the kind I grew up in. I'd always felt that the ghetto makes you tough and strong—unless it doesn't do anything for you at all but get you killed. I needed to have my girls around kids who were already where I was trying to take them. They had to learn to be rough, tough, and strong. Anyway, that was the main idea for moving to Compton. The result? I got more than I bargained for.

After two days in this hellhole, I was ready to move. I had never been in a war before. Here I was at forty-one years of age and I felt like I had been drafted into the U.S. Army and dropped into hostile territory. Near as I could tell, Compton was held by the enemy, and the president and his cabinet were members of the most notorious and ruthless gangs in the nation.

The president of Compton was 2-Evil, a young man about twenty years old. His destiny was to be a gang member. His father, Evil-One, and his mother, Angie-B, were gang members, too. When 2-Evil was just four years old, he helped his dad in a robbery. Using his small size, he crawled through a window and unlocked the door so his father and his homeboys could rob the place. This was just the beginning of his downward spiral in and out of juvenile detention centers for crimes ranging from petty theft and burglary to strong-arm robbery.

A street-smart, high-ranking member of the Bloods and always a step ahead of the police, 2-Evil ruled Compton. He used drugs like weapons. Rock cocaine was an explosive device and heroin turned heroes into zeroes. PCP was the mind destroyer, a drug so powerful it could tranquilize an elephant. It was one of the worst drugs on the street, and yet young men and women took it for breakfast, lunch, and dinner, slowly destroying their minds and, ultimately, their lives.

There was no law and order in Compton. A little black girl was shot in the back of the head by a storeowner who killed her for stealing a bottle of orange juice. Commerce was warfare. It was impossible to free the city from control by the Crips and Bloods, who occupied it like a military force. Crime was central to life here.

It took me only a couple of months to realize I was in the middle of hell and only God could help me now. I prayed without ceasing. I prayed hard that gangs would not kill my children. I cried to the Lord, "The Lord is my shepherd, I shall not want." Despite my prayer, I did want. I was not content. I wanted to run. Yet, I wanted things to change. I wanted to make a difference. I didn't know how. It was easy to see I would need the strength of Samson, the courage of Daniel, the wisdom of Solomon, and the power of Almighty God to fight the gangs that infested Compton.

In the depths of my heart, I wished God would rain down brimstone and fire and totally consume every gang member and cast them into the pits of hell. Maybe the police could line them all up and sentence them to death by firing squad. Kill all of the bastards. Was I insane? Were these the thoughts of a rational man? How could a man of kindness and humility change so quickly?

I hated President 2-Evil. He loved to ride in the neighborhood in his chauffeur-driven limousine. A crowd always surrounded the car and treated him like a foreign diplomat, which he was, because he was from East Compton. He was the government, and he got more respect in Compton than the president got in Washington. His bodyguards packed weapons and were not afraid to use them. They had an arsenal the LAPD was unable to match. To command respect, the bodyguards fired off rounds to see people crawl on their knees for safety. Many times, I was one of those helpless people desperately trying to escape the fire.

Nobody in Compton was prepared to deal with the gangs because it was just too easy to get killed. Blacks, whites, Mexicans, teachers, preachers, deacons, church members, city officials, the police, and the sheriff's department—they all ignored the fact that Compton was in serious trouble. Many years before, I had battled the Ku Klux Klan, but this was going to be much tougher because I would be fighting my own people. Where did I start? Who would I get to help me? How could one man stand against a gangster militia? Was there anyone who gave a damn except me?

My crusade began in earnest. My goal was to see not one more child killed in Compton. City Councilwoman Patricia Moore did all she could to help me, and we got to be friends. She was a hard worker, and I really appreciated it, but little came of our efforts. I visited more than thirty preachers, the police department, city council members, and even the mayor, to no avail. The mayor got so aggravated by my visits, he told his secretary to tell me he wasn't in. My face became a familiar sight, but pleas for help were hopeless.

One day I saw the mayor in the car next to mine, stopped at a red light. I yelled out my window, "Why don't you try to stop the gangs from taking over Compton?"

At first, he just stared ahead as if he was afraid to look my way. I repeated the question, knowing he recognized me.

He replied angrily, "Keep going the way you're going and you're going to be taken over, too. There's nothing I can do. There's nothing *anyone* can do."

When the light turned green, he accelerated as if a gang member was chasing him. I pulled my car over and cried. It hurt me immensely to see such a lack of concern. I grew convinced nothing and no one could change Compton. I decided to get out of this killing field where blacks had no respect for their own humanity. I rented a U-Haul and raced home to get my family packed so we could leave immediately.

As we headed north on Long Beach Boulevard, I stopped at a light and looked over when a commotion started at a Mobil gas station. Suddenly, a young man was shot down before my eyes. It was senseless. I could barely believe it. Yet, at the very moment that ambulance and police sirens began to wail in the distance, I knew I could not leave Compton. I might die in the war zone because every evil force of hell existed all around me, but I couldn't run away and give up. Someone had to change the community. Someone had to give the children hope. I was willing to die to stay in hell. I would continue to run my security business and save money, not to move out of Compton, but to remain in it.

My decision to train my daughters on the courts of Compton was a battle not only for tennis, but for my very life. Going to the park was like going to Wall Street where bankers did business. Unfortunately, instead of bonds and stocks, they were pushing rock cocaine. It was sold on every corner, in every market's parking lot. The street vendors sold hot dogs and hamburgers from their carts, and cocaine as a condiment. How could I train my daughters here?

Every day I left home, I didn't know if I would return. I kissed my wife and children as if each day was my last. I didn't know where to start but I knew City Hall was not going to help me. No one was on my side. After considering all my options and facing the fact there were none, I realized I had to free up the tennis courts in the local park so I could proceed with my plan to train my daughters to be the greatest tennis players who ever lived.

I went to Paramount Sports, owned by Ted and Bill Hodges, where I always bought used balls, and bought three hundred more for thirty dollars. I wanted to use old balls to train the girls, ones without much bounce, so they would have to build up the speed to get to anything. They didn't know a new ball from an old ball, so it wouldn't bother them. They'd have to generate their own power and run even harder, just like I did when I was fleeing white people in the South. I also bought twenty-nine Cobra racquets made by Wilson and some big Prince racquets. I added some racquets from a company called Yonex to my supply. When certain models were discontinued, the store drilled holes in them so they would break if you hit a ball. For almost nothing, I bought a bunch to use for swinging practice.

I now had almost all the parts of the plan. I had studied tennis and mastered the game. My daughters were strong and healthy and ready to be trained. I had the environment to make the girls tough. I had the equipment and the training plan that I was now putting into effect. Only one more thing remained—a place to play.

I needed tennis courts I could use whenever I wanted, for as long as I wanted—and I wanted them to be free. There was a gentleman named James Powers who taught at Inglewood High School in Inglewood, California. I knew him from when I was learning to play. His sister worked at the park in Compton where there were abandoned tennis courts. They had broken glass all over them. They were dirty. There was human waste on them, along with needles, condoms, and anything else you could think of that was filthy or contaminated. They were exactly what I needed.

I asked James's sister if I could clean them up and use them.

She said, "If you can get on the courts, you can use them as much as you want to."

I immediately got a broom to sweep them, and used a hose to wash them, but hygiene was not my biggest problem. My problem was the gang members. This was their area to sell drugs, and the territory all around the tennis courts was theirs. Perhaps naïvely, after I cleaned the courts, I asked them to move elsewhere so we could use them.

"No, man, we ain't movin'," they told me flatly.

The more I talked to them, the more they insisted they weren't going anywhere. I said, "Well, someone is going to have to take the tennis courts from you, then."

"It won't do no good to call the police," they told me, smiling.

In this, they were right. Calling the police was useless. The relationship between the gangs and the police was one of indifference, corruption, and crime. Most cops' attitude was "let the niggers take care of themselves." I believed they were paid off from drug profits, so there was no profit in interfering. Gang members had Tec-9s and other automatic weapons. They didn't mind shooting you, either. Unlike the cops, they had no paperwork to fill out, or citizen review boards to worry about.

In the process of trying to get the gang members to move on, I got my teeth knocked out, my nose broken, my jaw broken, and my fingers dislocated. I took a beating almost every day. They beat me so badly I could barely walk, but I kept on coming back until they finally started saying, "Old man, do anything hurt you?"

I said, "Yeah, I hurt, but damn if I'm going."

"You better go," they warned me.

I said, "I'll be back tomorrow."

And every day I'd go back.

A year later, I had not gained any ground. The gangs were still in charge of the park, still selling drugs. My activity was stressing out my family. The children were constantly asking, "Why do you hang in the streets so much, Daddy? Why do you take a stick with a piece of pipe on the tip everywhere you go? Why do you come home with blood on your clothes? Why is your head always wrapped in white bandages? Why do you wear shades in the house?"

My explanations always upset them, especially Oracene. She was totally against my risking my life in Compton.

"Richard, what about your family? What are we going to do if something happens to you while you're out there fighting with gangs? You're too old for that. If they won't let you use the court, go somewhere else. Let's move out of this crazy place."

My response was simple. "Nothing can hurt me because God is on my side."

Disgusted, she said, "Let's see if God is on your side when they're kicking in your ribs."

Trying to teach tennis and help the people in the community was a full-time job, but I had to find a way to do it. As always, my security company was a perfect business for me. I could provide a valuable service, make money, and create my own schedule to work with Venus and Serena.

My security firm had a contract with a check-cashing business, and the owner paid me to provide security. Security meant something quite different in Compton than most places. Sometimes, while checking on my men guarding the building, we'd have to jump into an old steel shed where they kept pipes and construction materials because gang members doing target practice shot their automatic weapons and bullets came flying by.

One evening at work, I realized I had forgotten to go to the pharmacy to pick up some medication. Just after dark, I saw an old black man walking down my side of the street. He was probably in his late sixties. He looked honest and was decently dressed, and I thought he might help me. I stepped out from the building and said, "Excuse me, sir?"

As soon as I spoke, he crossed over to the other side of the road.

I caught up to him and said, "Why are you dodging me? I never did anything to you."

He said, "Son, where I come from in Alabama, you see a black man, you get yourself happy. Now when I see one it scares the livin' shit outta me. And you black."

I felt bad. I said, "I understand what you're going through, but I'm not that way."

He shook his head sadly. "Well, I won't take the chance."

That's how frightened he was, that was the climate of fear. What made it worse was we were all black. We were doing it to each other in the same race, within the same community. Hurt and violence was not an outside threat anymore. It was *us*.

It was the only time I was ever ashamed to be black.

It was a dark time, for sure. Why was it so hard to live among my own people? One night when I was checking my security guards, I saw a building on fire on Wilmington near Compton Boulevard. I ran up and saw the owner just watching it burn. Like a fool, I started to run to call the police and fire department.

He said, "Hey, wait. Whatever you do, don't stop it."

"Don't stop it?" I repeated, shocked.

He shook his head. "If you do, I lose money."

It took me a moment to realize he was letting it burn for the insurance money. That was Compton.

Yet, the truth was that a spark of ambition also lay under the surface, dying to get out. It was part of why I stayed. I knew two young men who were coming up strong. They vowed they would someday gain world attention. One was a boy called Eazy-E. The other was called Snoop Dogg. They sold their records from the Thrifty Drugstore and out of the backs of their cars to the neighborhood people. It made me see that no matter how much I thought I was the only one trying to do something in the neighborhood, other people were, too. There were young people with aspirations, wishing to break free and refusing not to try.

I spent a lot of time building relationships with the gang members. Learning to talk to them and listening to them. In some ways, I was a bit of a father figure. Most had never known one. Many of them reminded me of the time when I was much younger and just living to die, caring about nothing, convinced the future held nothing but my doom. Their eyes were dead, without hope. Yet, as different as we were, a fragile trust began to grow. It made things a bit easier, but never easy. It was commonplace for me to get to know a young man, only to have him disappear soon after, and be told when I asked where he was that he was dead.

I wanted to start working with Venus on the Compton tennis courts when she was five years old, but I realized the park was still too dangerous. I had to find a way to persuade the gang members to release their hold on it. It was an impossible task but one I had to accomplish. I went to the park every day. Drug transactions were continuous. Buyers came on bikes, motorcycles, and cars, and on foot, from the best neighborhoods to the worst. There was a drug empire operating in the heart of Compton and the park was its main headquarters, their Main Street. Asking the gang to give up part of the park was asking for a death sentence.

After many months of ineffective negotiating and getting into arguments and fights, I decided to take Venus to the tennis courts anyway. She was past five and already way behind in her training. Going to the courts was a risk I had to be willing to take. Feeling a little apprehensive, I took my broomstick with me just in case. It was three feet long, with a four-inch piece of steel pipe stuck on the end. Cracking one of those gangbangers across the head was not a problem for me if it protected us.

Venus and I walked through the park holding hands and singing. She was aware of the gang activity in the park, because drugs were sold everywhere in the neighborhood, including right in front of our house. While I was showing Venus how to swing her racquet, two rival gang members got into a fight outside the court. One of them pulled a knife, stabbed the other one, and then started kicking him. Everyone else retreated. It was obvious no one was going to stop them. I tried to ignore it and keep pitching balls over the net to Venus. Suddenly, she motioned me close.

"Daddy, why are those men cutting each other up?" she asked innocently. "Is this where you get cut up?"

"Venus, I'll explain that to you when we get home. Stay here on the court. I'll be right back."

With a quizzical look in her eyes, Venus held her racquet against her chest and stood by the fence. I grabbed my broomstick and walked over to the fight. For a moment, I hesitated. I looked back at Venus. I kept telling myself, "She will be okay."

My life had turned into a game of Russian roulette and it was only a matter of time before the hammer struck the wrong chamber. The fight was none of my business, but I felt a need to stop it, to get involved. People had crowded all around them but no one dared say a word or intervene. It was important to set an example. Black people could help black people, not just hurt them. As I went to break it up, a flashback exploded in my mind. Back in Shreveport, I had been stabbed trying to break up a fight just like this. Since then, I learned never to step between two people fighting. It always left your back exposed and made you an easy target.

The gang member was still kicking his fallen enemy. Making my way through the crowd, I appealed to his better nature. "Come on, young man. You can't keep kicking a man when he's down. He's had enough."

"Yeah, whatever, old man. Next time, I'm gonna stomp that nigger's brains out." He looked at the kid on the ground. "Let that be a lesson to you. Don't fuck with me." He kicked him again and walked away, laughing and joking with his homeboys.

I said, "Somebody go call the police."

The young man was bleeding from his chest. The left side of his face was swollen and blood spilled from the side of his head. Three of his teeth were on the ground, coated in blood.

He moaned. "Thank you."

I went back on the court and hit balls to Venus. I waited for the sound of the ambulance but it never came. Fifteen minutes later, I looked over to where I left the kid. He was gone. No ambulance, no police, and no police report. This would be settled on the streets.

Venus and I stayed on the court for an hour. After practice, we picked up the balls, the racquets, and my broomstick. We walked hand in hand through the park. When we approached where the fight had taken place she said, "Oh, Daddy, you're so brave. The other people were scared, but not my daddy. I'm gonna be just like you when I grow up."

I asked, "What do you mean by that, Venus?"

She answered, "I'm going to be the champion of tennis and queen of the court. No one will ever be able to beat me, just like they can't beat you."

I laughed aloud, lightly squeezed Venus's hand, and walked home.

Maybe all those cuts and bruises I carried were worth it.

Two weeks later I was on the court with Venus and saw three gang members take an old man's walker from him just outside the gate. He just stood there. He couldn't move without his walker. It brought tears of rage to my eyes. Finally, helpless, the old man fell to the ground and the gang members just left him there.

I told Venus sternly, "Sit down until I come back."

I ran up to the gang members to ask them to give the walker back, or give it to me and I would give it back.

"Why did you take his walker?" I asked.

One answered, "I was gonna rob him but he didn't have any money, man. I can sell this for a few dollars and get me some stuff."

I said, "Give that man his walker back."

He said, "Nigger, I'll give you my foot in your ass."

So I said, "Tell you what, I give you my foot first," and I went to take the walker from him and the two other kids.

The three of them jumped me. They shoved me. They punched me. I lost my balance, fell to the ground, and they started kicking me. I could hear Venus's small voice in the background yelling, "Don't hit my daddy." After it was over, I picked myself up and headed for Venus. Why had I tried to stop them? The same reason I had for staying in Compton—an old man on a walker who couldn't do anything but stand there when the gang members took it.

I helped the old man to his feet. Then I got Venus, collected our gear, and walked the old man to our old Volkswagen bus. I said, "Sir, I'll have another walker for you before the day is over."

Hopelessness is a heavy weight on your shoulders, sometimes too heavy to carry. I saw it in the old man's eyes. I felt it inside me. I wanted it away from Venus, worried it could infect her like a disease. I was humiliated. No father wants his child to see him beat up. But Venus saw things her way.

She said, "Daddy, you can really fight. I want a heart like yours. I want to be just like you, Daddy."

I neglected to mention that *winning* might be the better goal for her, and just shook my head. "Venus, I don't ever want to see you fighting like I was doing. I don't ever want you around dangerous criminals. I just want you to work on your tennis and get the best education that's possible."

She looked at me with a devilish grin and said, "I want to get me some boxing gloves so I can learn how to fight just like you."

I took the old man home and then we went home. I told Oracene what happened and that I intended to replace the walker. She wasn't happy, but when I made my mind up about something, there was no stopping me. I went door to door through the neighborhood collecting money. People in the neighborhood were very understanding, and after a few hours, I had enough for a new one. I put the money in an envelope, drove to the old man's house, and slid the envelope under the door.

The training continued. Every day I took Venus to the court to work out. Serena always wanted to go along because she and Venus were so close, a bond that would last a lifetime. I was afraid to bring them at first, but soon began a routine of taking both girls to the court. For a while, things were okay, but it was just a matter of time before a confrontation took place.

In December 1985, alone, I got the worst Christmas gift I ever received. In my continuing effort to get the gangs to stay away from the courts, I got into a fight with six or seven gang members. To this day, the details are hazy, but I do remember when I woke up that ten of my teeth were missing from being kicked in the mouth. Over the years, I have grown accustomed to not having teeth, and to this day wear my "toothlessness" as a badge of courage. On top of that, however, I had a sprained arm and broken ribs. Breathing caused me excruciating pain. I had to go to the hospital to be treated. It was embarrassing—black eyes, broken ribs, missing teeth, and swollen jaw. To make matters worse, the tires on my Volkswagen bus were slashed and the windshield smashed. How could I go home this way?

I looked around. My tennis balls were scattered everywhere and my racquets were cracked. I was lost. My dreams were smashed like my body. How could I face my family? I thought things over. It took a while for me to see the bright side of things, but I decided I came out ahead. I was alive. However, I wasn't able to go to the tennis court for weeks. Days seemed like months as they dragged by. Anxiety consumed me. Every night I would lie awake in bed thinking about all the money I had to spend to fix my bus and replace the balls and racquets. I stayed awake plotting my revenge.

The day would come when I would return to the courts.

Finally, I was able to go back, but this time I didn't take Venus and Serena. Instead, I took my twelve-gauge pump shotgun. Nothing's as scary as the *click-chunk* sound of that pump driving a shell into the breech. I drove up to the court and saw some of the gang members that had beat me up selling drugs. They had stomped the teeth out of my mouth. They had kicked me in the head and broken my ribs without hesitation or remorse. Enough was enough. I couldn't take any more. Not one more day. It was the second time in my life I was too damn tired to stand it. I was too tired of fighting. My shoulders couldn't carry the weight any longer. My mind couldn't fight the fury. I was worn out and worn down. My life in Compton was a nightmare. The arguments, the fights, the beatings—they were torture. I was about to end it, or end someone's life.

I stepped out of the VW. The gang members saw the shotgun and took off. I was disgusted and filled with rage. I went hunting and I do believe I would have killed every one of them that day if I had found them. Finally, exhausted, I went back to my VW and proceeded home. It took a while; there were police cars and an ambulance on Atlantic Avenue blocking traffic. I parked the VW to look at the cause. Lying dead in the middle of the street was one of the gang members who had beaten me. Gathered around his body were his friends and family. I heard the screams and cries of his loved ones. There was so much grief and pain. I had no idea what had happened, but at that moment, I knew I never wanted to cause that type of pain. I promised myself I would never take the shotgun out again. I did not want to kill anyone. If I got beat up again, they might kill me, but I would rather have that than kill one of them.

The next day I got to the tennis court, they were waiting for me. I went up to the gang leader and said, "You know, you're much younger than I am; you think you could beat me?"

He said, "I'll be honest with you, I'm scared of you. Man, if I start shootin' you in your ass or hurt you, you the kind of a nigger could die, come back, and hurt someone."

"No one's comin' back," I said.

He just looked at me. We both knew where it was going. I wanted the court. He wanted the court.

"Why don't you and I *do* this?" I said. "And if you see I'm getting the best of you . . . ," and before he could answer, I started to fight. I beat him for everything I was worth, until he started yelling, "Man, get this old devil off me. Get this old devil off me. Stop it, man."

His boys pulled us apart. I didn't have to say anything. He and I both knew he would have to shoot me. It would take that to stop me.

He shrugged and walked off, and his boys followed. Was it respect, or indifference, or just convenience? I would never know.

It had taken two years and almost destroyed my body and my spirit. But in that moment, none of that mattered.

What mattered was the courts were ours.

CHAPTER **NINETEEN**

I started stockpiling every extra penny I earned to pay for the girls' training or for an emergency. I didn't want, nor did I ever seek, the kind of endorsements other parents wished for their children. If I was going to put my kids into tennis, it was my responsibility to outfit them and train them. What we didn't have, we did without, willingly. We were one family, devoted to each other, with one goal, supporting each other as we went forward.

It wasn't our nature to worry about what others thought of our coming from the ghetto, or spend a lot of time comparing ourselves to others. Serena remembers it this way: "When you're a little kid, you don't think about rich and poor, so I never really thought about what I had or didn't have. I just knew I was alive and had fun and did what my parents told me. I was happy. I never felt like I wanted things I couldn't have. I never had a bed until I was ten, but I always shared one with my sisters, or slept with my parents. It was fun sleeping with my sisters, especially Venus, because we were so close. As the youngest, you just slide around a little bit because people don't take as much notice of you. When your older sisters get in trouble, you don't.

"My dad was definitely strict when we were young. We had to study every night and do our journals and go to bed every night at nine o'clock. Venus would always read to me and we'd talk for hours. When I couldn't sleep, she would tell me stories. Every time, as soon as she started telling me a story, I would fall asleep. A second into the story, I would be asleep, but if she didn't tell me a story, I couldn't sleep.

"I really looked up to my dad. I was a daddy's girl. I think girls with both parents are usually daddy's girls, and most boys are mama's boys, but, of course, we didn't have any boys that lived in the house with us. I just remember my dad was so tall to me, my head was always below his butt. I never could get beyond the height of his butt. I don't know why it sticks in my memory. I just remember thinking, one day I want to be taller than his behind."

Training started early for my kids, but it wasn't only on the tennis courts. I used to take Venus and Serena to work with me so they could learn the importance of planning, responsibility, and a strong work ethic, even at their early age. In my final seventy-five-page plan, I called this program the Job Development and Education Preparation (JDEP). I bought dozens of books for the girls so they would have something to do when I took them to work with me. They loved reading and thought they were the best readers in the entire world. It amazed me how much they learned from one day to the next.

The women in our neighborhood saw me take the girls to work, and knew my stress on reading. When they started comparing me to their husbands, I knew I was going to have a problem.

"Why don't you spend your time with our children like Richard Williams? A good father cares if his children can read. If he can take his girls to work with him, why can't you?"

This attitude contributed to some of the men being jealous of me. It eventually escalated into anger. In retaliation, they set fire to a building I was protecting on Compton Avenue. I was so angry I tried my best to catch them and break their necks. As usual, the building's owner did not share my sentiment. He gladly collected the insurance payout.

Neighbors thought I was working the girls too hard. They didn't like that from the time Venus and Serena were three and two, I had them delivering phone books in the neighborhood for money. But little Serena's attitude was one of combat even then. "I wanted to pick up the phone books all by myself and my dad wouldn't always let me because they were so big and heavy. At two, I was really small, the runt of the family, and I remember those phone books being basically bigger than me, but I felt like, 'I can pick this book up.' In fact, I got angry because my dad only let me deliver one phone book. I said, 'I want to do more.' So me and Venus would drag the books across the lawns and up the steps and deliver them together."

Actually, their mom didn't like my taking such little ones to deliver phone books, either. She got so upset she decided to leave me. I lost a wonderful wife, I thought, till she got back to *her* mom's house and saw her lazy brothers doing nothing, and people around the neighborhood doing less. She came right back home and the girls kept on delivering phone books.

The difference between the way our family did things and the way the other people around us did things continued to increase. When Venus was nine years old, she made all As in school. So did Serena, because she had to do everything Venus did. Some of the neighborhood people made a fuss about my making the girls study so hard, and practice tennis for so many hours. Someone even called the police on me for abusing my kids.

I told the police, "I don't mind you coming and locking me up for that reason, but what won't happen is you damn cops coming here one day to tell me you're sorry you had to blow my daughters' damn heads off because they were on drugs or running around stealing cars or hanging with hoodlums. You won't ever tell me that."

I was not going to let my girls be swept into a culture of drugs and bad people. Too many young black girls in the ghetto got pregnant because they didn't have parents to make them avoid it, or thought it was the only thing a young black girl could do. For that reason, I didn't let my girls play with dolls. I had nothing against dolls. I just didn't want Venus or Serena to believe motherhood was the end goal of their lives when there were so many other goals to be attained.

I believed another way to prevent my children having bad values was to have them see reality firsthand. Venus was about six years old, right after my mom died, when I took her and Serena down to Skid Row in Los Angeles. People lived on the street there, and everything they owned was in a shopping cart. One lady was arguing, cursing, and drinking wine. I stopped the car for Venus and Serena to listen.

The lady came up to us and told Venus, "Give me a dollar."

Venus looked at her long and hard. Then she looked at me.

I said, "It's up to you,"

Richard teaches his daughters—Serena (left) and Venus (right)—how to golf. (Alese and Morton Pechter)

Honoring the city firefighters.

Venus celebrates her first
U.S. Open championship.
(Gregory Armstrong)

Mom, Oracene, celebrates victory with Venus and Serena.

Serena makes a midcourt volley.

Open stance forehand

Open stance forehand

Open stance backhand

Open stance backhand

The Williams Life Triangle

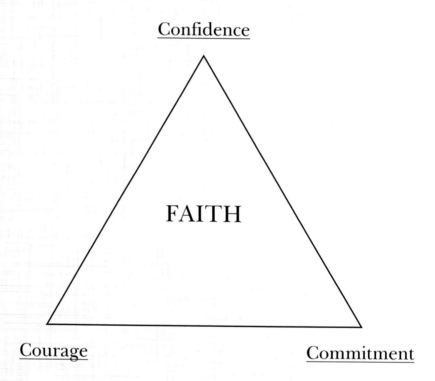

Confidence

FAITH

Courage   Commitment

BLACK AND WHITE213

She gave the lady a dollar and that lady started crying. She was close enough they could see the bugs in her hair. Before then, you couldn't get Serena to dress well or do her hair. After we left, from that day forward, Serena wanted to change clothes two or three times a day, and to this day you can't stop Serena from dressing up. She used to tell me, "I don't wanna live like those people."

That lady also told my girls she had a baby, somewhere. She said she never knew she was having sex, she was so high.

The girls asked, "Well, who's the baby's father?"

"I don't know."

"Well, when did it happen?"

"I don't know."

After that, I had to ask them, "Is this the life you want?"

"No, we don't want that life."

Then I took them to Beverly Hills and drove around and let them see things.

"Is this the life you're looking for?"

"Yes."

"Good. Then this is what you need to do."

Life is a firsthand experience. I tried to give my girls a special "life education." First, they had to learn that tennis was only a game. That's why they call it "playing" tennis. I wanted them to know that the life they lived off the court, their family life, was far more important. In the family, we cherished and loved one another. When people ask me how I got along so well with Venus and Serena, I tell them the key to getting along with your children is honesty. I was always honest about how much I loved being a father and enjoyed the responsibilities that came with it. I was honest with them about how I saw life. I was honest that they had to take responsibility for themselves. I was honest that Oracene and I would not accept anything but obedient children. I was honest about my mistakes. That made it easier for the kids to be honest with me. Venus and Serena always shared their real feelings with me. If Venus did something, she would tell me. If Serena did something, she would tell me. That has never changed.

I don't think you can prepare a child for life too early, but that's not what we do in America anymore. My mom used to say to me that I couldn't raise my kids the way they did in the forties and fifties. I thought she was wrong. Previous generations worked early, learned early, left the house early. Our children go to nursery school at three and learn to sit in a circle. They go to kindergarten at five years old and learn arts and crafts. In Europe and Asia, kids start early and go to class from seven in the morning till late in the afternoon, with one lunch break. That would not work here—it would be called child abuse. It's why we cannot compete with those countries.

I feel that we're way too soft on our children. The way Venus and Serena were raised, they didn't have any choice but to be strong. When they were five years old, they had to learn Tae Kwon Do to protect themselves. They also had to learn how to dance ballet and tap. Having taken dance lessons myself to learn to move better on the tennis court, I knew they would learn balance and grace the same way. It would also always be a positive part of their lives. I taught them about money and made sure they always worked to have their own. After school, they used to help each other sell lemonade and cookies outside on the sidewalk. They enjoyed it and made money, and they weren't even open on Sunday.

We're too soft on ourselves and our kids. We don't demand excellence. We don't train them to work hard from an early age. We want to give them kindergarten and ring-around-the-rosy and nonsense that does not really give you any security. Security comes from knowledge. Knowledge is power. Power is the ability to win.

That's what I believe. That's why I brought them up that way, and I always tried to be a good example for them. I believed that if *I* showed them I had strength of character, I would have more success creating children with character. If you are a parent, you should know this does not happen by accident. I did not just send the girls off on a bus somewhere, or to a class. I took them by the hand. I showed them the ghetto. I showed them Beverly Hills. I showed them the champions of their sport. I showed them struggle. I gave them a family history. I taught them about literature, philosophy, and the history of their race.

I told them, "I am a thinking man. You must be thinking women."

However, in my plan, making Venus and Serena tennis stars posed one question far more difficult and important than any other. *Was I going to be their father or their coach?* It went around and around in my mind. Could I be one to the exclusion of the other? Could I be both? What kind of parent would I be if I tried to be father *and* coach? I had studied tennis. I had trained Oracene. I knew how to succeed. But how could I transmit all that knowledge to Venus and Serena and take them through the daily grind of tennis training without blurring or damaging the most important role in my life and theirs—being their father? What would continual correction and criticism do to our relationship?

In all matters, including tennis, I decided I would always be their father first. I have never regretted my decision for an instant. What a relief it was to have that as my guide. In one stroke, I had removed from my life the burden of criticizing my children. It was the best decision I have ever made. I have seen so much damage in this world done by parents who take the other road. No matter the necessities of Venus and Serena's tennis training, or the goals I had set for them, I was their father first and they were put on this earth to be nurtured by me into fine and happy people. Tennis would be part of their lives, a big part, but only part. From the beginning, I decided that if people came to me later on and told me my daughters were great tennis players, I had failed. Success would be if they came up to me and said my daughters were great people.

Approaching the girls' upbringing as a parent and not a coach, I could see that success in life was the union of three fundamental elements: confidence, courage, and commitment. They formed what I call the Williams Life Triangle, the cornerstone of what I taught Venus and Serena.

The Williams Life Triangle

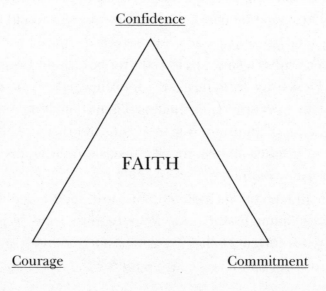

Confidence

FAITH

Courage   Commitment

The first and initially most important element of the tri-angle is commitment. How do we teach it? Always, by exam-ple. Teaching commitment to our children requires that we be models of commitment ourselves. We can't teach lessons to our children that we ourselves do not illustrate. A child best understands the theories of life his or her parents embody. We must be daily examples of the values we preach. To teach them strength, we must be strong. To teach them honesty, we must be honest. To teach them commitment, we must be committed.

My mother taught me about an important element of commitment-timing. When I was a child, I thought everyone got dressed up for church but me. I wanted a suit for church, too, so I went to make money by picking cotton. I picked all day for five or six weeks and saved enough money to get a suit. It was a good plan. I got a suit. The problem was that I forgot I needed a shirt, a tie, and shoes.

"Richard, you've done a great thing," Mama told me. "You have the suit you desire to have, but the commitment you had wasn't enough to follow through. You didn't do everything necessary to support it. The suit needed a shirt. The shirt needed a tie, and none of those things had you thought about."

I began to understand that a commitment was really a chal-lenge. Time is a factor in all challenges. I thought I'd go back and work twice as hard and buy the other things I needed, but the time wasn't there. Parents must teach children how to take advantage of time. If they have something or someone that takes away their time, it can also take away their commitment. If they are committed, they must let nothing stand in the way of their correct use of time.

I also found that it always helps to write notes on what you are committing to, and I had Venus and Serena do that from the time they were little. I got them in the habit of writing down their dreams and aspirations, and how they planned to reach them. They didn't have to write about tennis. In fact, I preferred they didn't. It could be a goal in school, something they wanted to learn, anything. I'd always find some special time to sit with each of them and help them write down on paper what they planned to accomplish that week. I think it's a great way to teach your kids to focus on their commitments and to measure their success. To this day, both girls keep journals and Serena keeps her "Tournament Journal" and her "Match Notes" in which she writes inspirational observations to herself before every match.

Serena once said to me, "Daddy, you know what I wanna be when I grow up?"

I said, "What?"

"I wanna be a veterinarian."

She wanted to be a veterinarian so much, she started surrounding herself with the things that would help her to be a veterinarian. I had her make notes on how to become a veterinarian. She wrote pages on the subject. She read books. She asked me to take her to see a veterinarian I knew.

I thought, *One day, boy, she's gonna be a great veterinarian.*

Of course, she changed her mind and became something far different, but it was the earliest commitment I saw her make and I was proud and impressed by her serious effort.

Of course, you don't always know what your kids are thinking—and it may be years before they tell you, like Serena did, and I had to laugh with her at what she said. "Dad, you *always* wanted to talk. The ten-page-plan writing assignments—you would take one topic and talk for hours. And hours. We would have family meetings, and you have to remember how little I was, so I kind of loved and hated them. Every time we sat down, you would say, 'If you fail to plan,

you plan to fail,' and, 'Serena, did you write down your plan?'
On and on. I always wrote something, even if I didn't actually mean it. It's funny, when you're young, you don't see
the value in it. You just don't want to sit there for two hours,
literally, two hours, and I'm gonna be honest, Dad, I wasn't
always listening. It's only now I see the real value of learning
how to plan and organizing my thoughts. Now I understand
how important those lessons were, and what part they play in
life. The love of your family, that's what's important. Knowing that you are loved and that you created love in others,
that's what's real."

One advantage I had with Serena was having Venus as a role
model. Venus was the greatest example of true commitment.
Venus is the most committed person I have ever known. I was
happy Serena looked up to her. I wanted both girls' heroes to
be their sisters and parents, the ones who loved and cared for
them.

Venus's first commitment was to reading. I wanted her to
read everything she could lay her hands on—and she did just
that. To this day, she has never stopped reading. She always
surprises me. She's a really unbelievable human being. Sometimes, I'd check on the kids around midnight, after putting
Venus in bed by nine, and she was still reading. She got Serena to read, too, and loved explaining things to her. Serena
still demonstrates the awesome commitment she learned from
Venus, in the work she does and the life she leads.

The truth is, I have never met a child who failed on his or
her own. Bad friends, bad families, bad neighborhoods, all too
easily stand in the way of a child's commitment to success. This
is why you find that the children who understand commitment

almost always have a model for it. My mother was my model. She raised me and taught me. I tried to emulate her love and her strength of character. I tried to be my children's model by having good character myself, by being honest with them, by being positive, by succeeding in business, by owning property, and by being so clear about my love.

When Oracene was pregnant, she meant so much to me I wanted to be there with her all the time and go through everything she went through. I knew I couldn't physically feel the pain of the load she was carrying, but mentally I thought I could. When she went to the doctor, I would go also, not one time, every time. I refused to leave her side, even when the doctor was examining her. It got so the doctor up and told me to go into the waiting room. To be polite, I agreed, but I didn't go. The next time he told me I needed to go to the waiting room, I said, "I sure will if that's where you're gonna do your examination. But if you're not, you better stop asking me to go out there because I'm gonna stay right here with her."

As we got closer to Venus's birth, it seemed like every three or four days Oracene would go to the hospital. Finally, they said she was ready to deliver, and I took her to have Venus. As I was putting on the gown and slippers to go to the labor room, I started thinking about all the things I wanted Venus to do—to play tennis, to be educated, to be a certain kind of person. Then I thought about what that little baby was going to experience if she was going to do all that. She was going to go through all of the prejudice I had been through. She was going to be called names. She was going to be called "nigger." I could visualize it all, and I didn't want that for my child. Suddenly, I couldn't bear for Venus to come into this world. Not that I didn't love her. Of course I did. I didn't love what she would have to go through—and if there was any way I could have stopped it, I would have. I started to yell. Pain tightened my chest and sweat poured off me like I was having a massive heart attack. My life rose up to haunt me and I couldn't bear my child having to go through what I experienced. The nurses wanted to know what was wrong, but I couldn't share with them what was happening inside me.

It turned out Oracene was having a false labor, so I calmed myself down and we headed back home. On the way, she asked me, "Did you hear some fool hollering his head off in the hallway? He was yelling and screaming and disturbing everyone."

I didn't want to tell her that fool was me.

When we got home, I made her as comfortable as I could and went out and walked for a while. I was so scared and nervous I started praying, asking, "Jehovah, don't never ever let me have fear again. Take my fear from me." That night, I felt my fear leave me and not return. I vowed that what had happened to me was never going to happen to my children. Venus once told the press, "My dad, when we first came up, he couldn't say what was on his mind or what he was thinking."

For the record, that's what was on my mind, and what I have always been thinking.

CHAPTER **TWENTY**

He would grant you according to the riches
of his glory, to be strengthened with
might through his Spirit in the inner man.

EPHESIANS 3:16

Moving to Compton and taking the courts back from the gangs showed the family the strength of my commitment. When I got beat up in front of Venus by those guys in the park, I felt terrible, but it made Venus's commitment to me even stronger. It amazed me that she learned you could stand up and put your best foot forward no matter what happened.

"Daddy," she said, "you know, one time I didn't wanna come to this park no more."

I said, "Well, maybe we won't. I'm not sure I want to go through this again."

Venus planted her hands on her hips defiantly. "Oh, no. We are coming back tomorrow."

"You wanna come back tomorrow and watch me get beat up?"

She shook her head firmly. "Oh, you won, didn't you know that?"

I had to laugh. "Yeah, they got so tired of beating on me they needed a rest."

Every now and then, we still laugh about it.

No, Daddy, you won . . .

It is important that parents show their kids they are worthy of the child's commitment, but here's the most important part—it must be the child who is committed. I will say it again. A parent must let the *child* be committed. Don't be committed for them. I've seen parents give their children the best clothes, the best shoes, the best racquets, and drive them around in Mercedeses and Rollses. But when the children grew up, they were not committed. It had all come too easily.

I saw kids out there in junior tennis I thought were better than Venus and Serena, but because of their parents' over-commitment, the child did not follow through. There was one boy who was on the road to being a professional tennis player. I called him the "Can't Miss Child." He can't miss. It's certain. He's going to be a professional. But for all his promise, he never made it. When he had to play, he said, "I'm not accustomed to bringing my own water." His parents used to get the water for him.

"I don't wanna carry this bag, it's too heavy."

His parents always carried the bags.

When he needed self-motivation, he didn't have it. His parents always motivated him, so when he was alone, his motivation failed. A parent can be a guide, someone to get them through the jungle. Show them how to get to their destination, but don't bring them to it. You can't carry them. It will not be good for the child.

The other important thing about commitment is that it cannot be taught if you are unwilling to risk failure. If you are so worried your children cannot handle failure, you have no faith in their character. Failure is instructive. They must be allowed to fail so they learn how to pick themselves up again. If the only way to make sure your children succeed is to do everything for them, they will surely fail as soon as you're not there. Mental toughness comes from realizing failure is just a way of learning what more you need to know.

Once I taught tennis to a girl with a problem. The problem was her mom. When the girl got sick, her mom was there. The girl ran short of money, her mom was there. If she wanted to go out and she didn't have a ride, she called her mom. The mom never even thought about saying no. When the girl left to go to USC, she made it through because mom did all the homework. Mom was also the first one to say she didn't know why her child didn't make it as a tennis player. The child *couldn't* make it. She didn't have a chance because she never learned to make her own commitment. Her mom had done everything for her and, by doing so, had stood in her way.

We overdo it in America when it comes to being committed to our children. We have to allow our children to be committed to themselves. Venus and Serena learned about commitment because they wanted to succeed. They lived in Compton. They came out of the ghetto. They saw kids carrying guns like schoolbooks. They had to take life seriously. It was the same way when I was a child in Shreveport. I had to be committed to myself. I had to know when and where and how fast to run, and how far. There was real danger. The enemies were genuine. I nurtured commitment in Venus and Serena the same way—by making them take responsibility for themselves.

When Venus was fourteen years old, we went to Oakland to play her first professional tennis tournament, the Bank of the

West Classic. She was so excited she couldn't wait to leave the hotel room for her match.

"Let's go, let's go," she kept insisting.

"Venus, do you have everything?" I asked her.

"Oh, yeah. I'm ready, Daddy."

The child had a smile on her like a hyena ready to pounce, but her tennis dress was on top of the TV and she didn't see it.

I asked her three times, "You sure you have everything?"

"Oh, sure, Dad, I'm sure. Let's go."

"You checked your bag?"

"Sure, let's go, Daddy."

I nodded. "Okay. Let's go, then, Venus."

We walked out the door with her dress still sitting up there on the TV. She had left it. I thought about it all the way to the tournament. When we got on the practice court and started hitting, I thought, *I guess she's going to play her match in those shorts she has on.*

Abruptly, Venus stopped hitting the ball and called me to the net.

"You know what?" she began nervously.

"Let me tell you what," I said. "You left your dress on top of the TV."

She was shocked. "You knew it?"

I said, "Yeah, I knew it."

"Well, why didn't you say something?" she demanded.

"It was not my responsibility. It was yours," I said, and she started crying.

Tears came pouring out of her eyes as she ran as fast as she could to the tournament referee. Of course, Venus had been getting so much media attention, the tournament officials wanted her to play. They even tried to get a police car to take her back faster to the hotel while they delayed her match.

I didn't agree.

"She plays at seven," I insisted, quite relaxed about it all. "It's after seven. She defaults. You have to teach her a lesson."

Unfortunately, the WTA wasn't about to cut Venus Williams, but I would have had no trouble if they did. I still think they should have. Fortunately, a close call was enough. Venus learned her lesson. From that day forward, she was committed to packing her clothes correctly. I didn't have to tell her anything. She put together a check-off list and began using it, and does the same thing to this day.

If I had been committed for her, and told her about the dress, it would have never had the same effect as her leaving it home and suffering the consequences. I'd have been like most of the parents of the girls and boys I see out there right now, who can't manage their own affairs or be committed on their own. You can be committed *to* your child. You cannot be committed *for* your child. It is impossible for a child to be mentally strong if you are committed for them. A child without commitment will not grow up to be a responsible person because the responsibility left that child many years ago.

We're making a mistake if we want to do more for our kids than what was done for us, whether we're rich or poor. Allow your children to make their own commitments. Let them earn it. Let them make mistakes. Mistakes are rarely harmful, and especially not at an early age. Once, I let Isha drive the family car at age twelve, when we were delivering phone books. She ground up the gears and hit several parked cars and cost me a thousand dollars. I never raised my voice at her. However, as far as discipline and respect in our household went, Serena put it quite simply and accurately: "I always did what my parents told me to do. If my mom or my dad told me not to do something, I didn't do it. That's just how it was. There was no question. I just respected that and listened, and it was fine."

A scientist once told me that if I kept going the way I was going, my "daughters might be really, really great." I was also told by people that I was "going to run my daughters crazy" and "they're not going to like you." I took nobody's word. I taught them all the things my mom taught me. My mom was my hero, and I think I'm pretty close to being Venus and Serena's hero. Serena took that to heart. "I didn't want to feel like I ever failed my parents," she said. "Sometimes it's hard. I make decisions. Should I do that? Was I raised this way? Am I making a mistake? I'm the kind of a person that lives my life like that. My choices are very personal. I feel really fortunate. I've never felt like I needed something I didn't get. When I'm dating a guy, I don't think that I'm looking for something that my father lacked, because he had everything, and that's so great. I feel awesome that I don't need someone to fulfill a role that was never filled for me.

"When you're younger, as a female, you flock to your father. When you get older, you're closer to your mother. I still feel really, really close to my father, even though I'm older. We have a great relationship. There is an appreciation. There is a closeness because of what we've been through together, and a respect. Not only do I respect him, but I feel he respects me, which is weird, because I don't feel like he has to or he should. I think it shows a really humble attitude that he does."

The result? We get along great to this day. It is my happiest moment when my daughters call me and tell me they love me, or Serena dedicates her book to me, or when Venus sends me an email saying, simply, "Thank you, Daddy, for making me a champion," or when they simply say, "Hi,

Daddy," as a kind of sign-off, when they're interviewed after a victorious match.

No one can break us apart. We are a family. That's why I made the decision always to be their father and not their coach. Being a father can't be a losing position, ever. It was ridiculous when the media used to say my girls "could do so much better if Mr. Williams wasn't around them, if he didn't take up for them." How could any father who loves his children fail to protect them? I could never be a coward to my children, as my father was to me. I smile when I see the strength in my daughters. This generation is never going to have to crawl in the dirt the way my mother's generation did, wasting away in the cotton fields or working as janitors.

I raised warriors.

To toughen the girls' "skin," I used to bring busloads of kids from the local schools into Compton to surround the courts while Venus and Serena practiced. I had the kids call them every curse word in the English language, including "nigger." I paid them to do it and told them to "do their worst." As a result, I never had to take up for my daughters on the court. Serena takes care of herself. Everyone knows it. She'll tell you, "Just get the hell out of my face," or, "I don't like what you did."

Venus learned another kind of strength. Everyone on the tour knows that if Venus challenges a call, she probably has right on her side, because she has a major-league commitment to the truth. In 1998, Venus was playing a match and the umpire called a ball out incorrectly. I've never seen Venus get upset except for that day. She said to the umpire, "I'm gonna tell you, you know that ball was in, the world knows that ball was in, and I know that ball was in, and I wouldn't stand here and tell you that ball was in unless it *was* in."

One call in a lifetime of tennis didn't mean much, but Venus's words echoed around the world, a proclamation of honesty and integrity, all the things she stands for and believes in.

All her life, Venus never missed an opportunity to show her commitment to honesty and loyalty. A week after losing the finals of the 1997 U.S. Open to Martina Hingis, she was supposed to play a much smaller tournament. She was so big and popular after the Open, the tournament officials questioned whether she would even show up.

She simply said, "I gave you my word that I'd be here."

That's Venus. She committed to that tournament and followed through. That's very important. If you make the commitment, you must follow through. Your commitment is you. Without a commitment, you're not very much in this life.

While we were in Germany, Venus went into a store. When she came out, she had the strangest look I'd ever seen on her face.

I said, "What's wrong with you?"

"That man said something I didn't like, Daddy."

"What did he say?"

"I don't know. He said it in German. I'm angry I couldn't understand it."

I taught them at an early age, it's up to you to learn things you don't know. It turned out the man was complimenting Venus on her tennis. That very day Venus bought a book on German to learn to speak it. Serena speaks French because when she was twelve, she decided she wanted to win the French Open and felt that people appreciate you more when you can speak their language.

I agreed. "Serena," I asked her, "do you really want to win

the French Open and learn French? Can you make a commitment to do that?"

She said she could. Some time later, we saw Jim Courier win the French Open and give part of his victory speech in French.

Serena said to me, "I know more words than that."

I said, "I didn't know you knew any French at all."

She said, "Oh, yeah. You remember you kept saying I could learn it? I went and got a book. I was gonna surprise you."

Unlike most parents of today, I did not immediately run out and buy her French lessons. I did not run out and enroll her in Berlitz. I simply said, "It's up to you. It's not my job to push you into these things, not if you're serious."

You've got to constantly measure children's seriousness about what they want. That's an important yardstick. You can see the serious nature of children if you watch them play. Children love to feel they can do something well on their own. Hey, I'm doing this without my dad wanting me to do this, my mom wanting me to do this. I was not about to get Venus a German book or Serena a French book. I wasn't about to get them any type of book. They were the ones who needed to keep elevating their lives. They had to realize the commitments they should make. I couldn't be doing it for them. You do something for a child, that's great, but somewhere along the line, the child has to start growing up and doing things for him- or herself.

Sports are a great way to teach confidence and self-reliance and can be a very positive influence on a young person's maturity, especially for girls. Changing from being a little girl to being a young woman can be a difficult time, but a great thing about female athletes is they can keep their minds on sports and not on distractions. According to Serena, "I don't remember my whole puberty because I was in sports. I just remember

I got really ugly for a minute, and then one day I woke up and I was much cuter. I was really ugly from twelve or thirteen. I was skinny. Maybe every girl thinks that. A lot of people preach sports are good for women, and I agree. It keeps your confidence up and you're not thinking about anything else. That helps when you start to date. I didn't date when I was a teen. We weren't really allowed to have boyfriends, and I didn't have one. But when I did start dating, my dad never took me aside and said, 'Now this is someone you shouldn't date,' or, 'You shouldn't do this.' He let me make my own decisions.

"I also think sports were good for the family. I was always on the courts with all my sisters around, and my mother and father. It was a comfort, not a competition. It sounds too good to be true, but that's the way we were raised. Being Jehovah's Witnesses, we weren't competing with each other. We were supposed to love each other, and inspire each other, and not bring each other down. We weren't allowed to argue and fight with our sisters. We wanted what was best for each other and helped each other work to get it."

Work is a great thing. There is nothing like the feeling of having earned something, as opposed to having it given to you. As a boy, I had no choice but to work. It made me strong and gave me pride in myself. I was sure it wouldn't hurt my kids to work the same way. Too many parents let their kids stick out their hand for everything they want. That doesn't encourage commitment. In my opinion, it takes commitment away from the child.

Even as toddlers, any money Venus and Serena earned went into their accounts. Some people said, back when they saw the girls struggle to pick up those heavy phone books, that's the meanest father in the world. I really didn't see it that way. I knew that one day they would want money. Making a commitment to it would help them buy, or save for, whatever they desired. That's important. A lot of people don't think teaching their kids about money is a good idea. I think it's one of the most important things you can do. I am very good with money. I used to manage the money of some top-notch basketball players. No one ever lost a penny with me. Not one. When Venus and Serena signed their first big sports contracts, deals worth upward of fifty million dollars, I made them sit at the same table as the agents and the lawyers through every negotiation until they understood every clause in every contract.

Having my own company and funding everything myself taught me a lot about the tennis business. People were so foolish with money it amazed me. I saw basketball players sign away their rights for their own clothes and shoes. I saw millionaire football players and boxers go broke. It was reported that former tennis star Arantxa Sánchez Vicario lost sixty million dollars through mismanagement by her parents. I didn't make those mistakes.

I could buy my daughters whatever they needed, so it wasn't hard to turn down all the initial sponsorship deals we were offered, or to tell the USTA we weren't going to play more than one or two of their tournaments a year. Or that staying in school was more important than the USTA's need for new stars, or that their favorite slogan for young players that "travel was educational" was never going to beat a real education.

John Evert, tennis great Chris Evert's brother, was an executive at International Management Group (IMG). He told me, "Mr. Williams, we can give you and your daughters shoes, clothes, or anything else you want."

I reminded him, "If you look at them, they have shoes on."

"How about racquets?"

I said, "That's how you heard about 'em, right? They have racquets."

I wouldn't let anyone give us a racquet for free. No one could give the girls shoes, either. I was committed to them.

Commitment requires a strong self-image. Accomplishments and goals are the essential building blocks of self-image. They are a big part of what makes my daughters who they are. I still smile thinking about three-year-old Venus and two-year-old Serena dragging those heavy books across a big yard and up onto the front porch. When people say, "Boy, those girls got muscles you won't believe," I guess I should respond, "You would, too, if you started wrestling phone books when you were two or three."

The older the girls got, the more they increased their commitment to saving money. Serena was five when she opened her first savings account. Venus already had one and Serena wanted to be exactly like her sister. They loved the independence money gave them, and soon realized there might be easier ways to earn it.

Venus used to love to go to Sears during Halloween, and both girls loved the Little Folks Shop at the Long Beach Mall. Using their own money, they bought their own clothes. Venus had an unusual way of looking at shopping. When she got the receipt for a purchase she called it a "per paid." As long as she had the "per paid," she thought she could take it back to the store and buy anything she wanted for that price. It wouldn't cost her anything because she already paid for it. I believe it set the tone for her and her sister to be the champion world-class shoppers they turned out to be.

Sometime around six years old, Venus asked me, "Daddy, why is it you don't work hard?"

I said, "I do work hard."

Venus pointed to my home office. "Dad, it looks like all you do is just sit down at that desk over there."

At that time, I still owned the security service and had men all over the city guarding businesses under contract to me. Both girls thought it was "really cool" that I called my business Samson Security, because Samson was in the Bible and, as Serena put it, "the strongest guy ever." I used to work late keeping track of my employees, servicing new accounts, and adhering to all the different laws we operated under. The paperwork was endless, but I could do most of it at night so it didn't interfere with teaching the girls. I knew the girls didn't understand the importance of writing contracts or sending out letters, but I liked their desire to go from being "manual phone book laborers" to my "easy" job of deskwork.

I said, "Venus, if you want a sit-down job all you need to do is get someone with a building to hire you to protect it, and then hire two guys to be guards, one inside and one outside, and you can sit in an air-conditioned office and make money."

She said, "You're kidding."

I said, "No."

"Show me, Daddy."

I was amazed she wanted to learn about business, but she made a commitment and that was that. She sat there half the night learning how my business worked. Today, both Venus and Serena have their own businesses. They have never lost money through neglect or failure to know what was going on. Serena attributes this to several things. "My dad always made us make our own decisions. He always made an effort to teach us about money and business. When I signed the Puma deal, I was at the table for every transaction and negotiation. I'm a really savvy businesswoman, and I learned a lot of that through him. We spent a lot of days and nights in the negotiation room, no matter how tired I was. I know he respects the fact that I never lost money, that my businesses run right, and I take care of all the people who I'm responsible for and who depend on me."

That's a great attitude. Unlike so many sports figures who lose their money through bad management or poor judgment, I know Venus and Serena will always be in charge of their businesses, their tennis, their relationships, and their lives. They have the confidence they learned from the time they were children. But commitment and confidence are only the first steps in being champions.

There is another truth I believe in totally.

Even a champion can falter without faith.

CHAPTER **TWENTY-ONE**

Be strong and of good courage, do not
fear nor be afraid of them; for the Lord
your God, He is the One who goes with
you. He will not leave you nor forsake you.

DEUTERONOMY 31:6

Faith is a belief in something unseen. We all have faith, in some sense, but how strong is your faith? When Venus was nine years old, she told me something that has impressed me to this day. She was number one in the girls' ten-year-old junior tennis division, and we were driving home from a tournament in our old Volkswagen bus.

She said, "You know, I'm very good in tennis, huh?"

"Yes."

"I'm number one."

"Yes, you're number one."

"You know, I could beat McEnroe."

At the time, John McEnroe was number four in the world, and much older than Venus, and a man, and a tennis genius, but she had faith that she could beat him. Faith gives you that kind of confidence. It is the inner strength that lets you believe in yourself and a positive outcome. It is the lack of fear of your opponent. It is the strength to seize the moment and play without fear. It is the depth inside you that you draw from to find peace. It is the certainty you will win.

"Yes, Venus, I believe you can beat him," I replied without hesitation.

Should I have made her humble? Should I have said, "Now, Venus, you don't know if you can beat him. And I don't think you *can* beat him because he's older and stronger, but maybe someday, honey . . ."? No. A lack of faith wouldn't have helped Venus. In fact, it would have gone against everything she was taught. According to the Bible, if you have enough faith, you can move mountains. If she really believed that, she had every reason to believe that she could beat a tennis champion like McEnroe.

When you believe in yourself, when you have a deep and all-abiding faith, you become an unbelievable person. You can do exactly what you say you can do. That's the type of faith Venus had even at nine, a complete faith, a total trust. I believe in my heart that women have more faith than men. My mom planted that in me. She made me believe not only in God, but also in women. I believe in women more than I do in men. Their faith is real. My mom told me that "women sometimes are the last ones to speak, but we're such great thinkers because of it."

I raised Venus and Serena with the faith my mom gave me, the idea that you can do anything you wish if you believe in your heart that you can. Venus believed in her heart that she could beat McEnroe when she was nine years old, and I think, if you asked her today if she could have beaten McEnroe then, even with the knowledge she has as an adult, I think she'd say, "Yes, easily."

The kind of faith that Venus and Serena had started with the love of their parents and the devotion we taught them. We nurtured them to believe in themselves. Their faith also came from the trials of people like my mom, their grandmother, who began the family tradition of women being able to accomplish anything. You want an example of the complete faith my mom had? When my little sister Faye took sick with pneumonia, the doctor gave up on her. He said she was going to die.

Mom told me, "She not gonna die."

Unsure, I said, "Okay."

"Sonny, I've been up for three days and three nights. I need to go to sleep. You watch her. If death comes, wake me up."

"Mama, who is death? What's it look like?"

She said, "You'll know it, Sonny." Then her eyes started rolling back in her head and she started shaking.

"Death is here," she said, and went to sleep.

About thirty minutes later, both of Faye's eyes went completely white.

"Mama, wake up, get up here. Get up."

She got up and prayed, and in no time, Faye was okay, her eyes clear and normal.

Mama told me, "Now, that's the faith we all should have in this house. If you had, you coulda done it, too."

One of the most important building blocks in Venus and Serena's life was being taught their family history. They were given their place in a tradition of faith and courage that included a grandmother who could pray their aunt back to life. I personally saw the faith that stemmed from my mom. Back in the sixties, I was dating a girl who worked in a chemical plant. When the day came that I told her I didn't want to date her any longer, she had so much rage she poisoned me. I was taken to Harbor General Hospital in Torrance, California, and my sister Penny called my mom in Shreveport to come to the hospital. When she got there I was awake, but the doctors told her I was at the end.

She asked them, "Have you done all you can do for him?"

"Yes, ma'am. We have."

"Is there anything else you can do?"

"There's nothing we can do. He's dying."

"In that case," she said, "take all them IVs out of him and all those bags and everything else."

They protested, but she insisted. When everything was removed, she came to my side. "Sonny, do you have faith that you believe you can get up and start walking today?"

In all honesty, I really didn't, but I didn't want to let Mom down.

I said, "Oh, yes, ma'am."

"Then get up."

She put one of my arms over her shoulder and the other over my sister's. "Sonny, do you believe with all the faith you have that God can have you walking this afternoon?"

"Yes, ma'am."

She said, "Now you need to put your faith together, and if you really put your faith together you be walking this afternoon."

I tried to believe I'd be walking that afternoon. I prayed as I never prayed before. That same afternoon, I was walking. The record is on file to this day, Harbor General Hospital, Richard Williams. Without my mom's faith, I would have perished. Hers was a woman's faith, a faith that men cannot touch. Women can do anything. I taught my girls that. I never gave them any sense that they were less than boys, that they weren't as good, or that they were inferior or subservient to anyone in any way. On this, there were no grays. Their strength was an article of faith, clear as black and white.

No child starts out bad. No child is born anything but good. Any time you see a bad child, you're seeing the home that child came from. Home brands a child forever. Home is where kids learn faith, or don't learn it. If you see a child doing drugs, go look at the home. If a child cheats and steals, go look at the home. If a child goes to jail, go look at the home. Long before Venus and Serena were born, I couldn't wait to teach them about the world, to give them faith in themselves, to make them champions. I even started talking to them about it when they were in their mother's womb.

Oracene used to say they didn't know what I was talking about.

I said, "If they don't know, how come they kick every time I'm talking?"

I wanted to teach Venus and Serena that being a woman wasn't a disadvantage, it was an advantage. I saw what women could do. I saw what my wife could do, what she was able to achieve, how she could make a home so happy, how she stood right by my side throughout everything in life. Even before we met, she was a very committed person with a strong faith.

I didn't have a dad or a brother, so I learned about strength from my mom. Oracene had the same kind of strength that she did. Beyond how beautiful she was physically, Oracene was equally strong as a person. You could feel the force of her faith inside her, and she inspired others with it. Her faith in what the girls could do stemmed from her faith in God. It really worked in her life.

One day, Oracene and the kids and I were at the park and I was a little upset with her. Now, I could really throw a baseball because I used to throw rocks in self-defense when I was a boy. She had a bat in her hand so I threw some balls at her and taunted her, saying, "I'm gonna strike you out so easy."

She kept insisting, "I don't wanna do this no more."

"I'm still gonna strike you out."

"And I still don't wanna do this."

The next ball I threw at her she hit over the fence.

Oracene's faith fit so well with me because I would not have allowed myself to be around someone who didn't have faith. I hope that she knows I believe that Venus and Serena couldn't have had a better parent, then and now. Oracene was centered in the tradition of strong women of faith. Her discipline did an awful lot to help me, and all of her kids. She's a unique and very wonderful person.

The highest compliment I can pay her is that she was just behind my mom in her faith. She just didn't have the same roots of struggle. When I was a kid, I heard an old lady named Miss Mattie had died, so I went to tell my mom.

Mom said, "She's not dead."

I thought Mom was crazy till they took Miss Mattie to the icehouse for the autopsy. Miss Mattie rose up and said, "What the hell you all tryin' to do?"

Oracene is wise in that same tradition, in a modern way.

What happened to us? Well, the power of money and success drives professional sports in America, and if you are not careful, you can easily succumb to it. Some deal well with wealth and find it easy to maintain their balance and stay on top. Others fall prey to the ugly side of fame and fortune and the invisible hand of pressure that accompanies it. The old saying is correct: "It's harder to stay on top than it is to get to the top."

I regret that the presence of so much success made it impossible for us to continue our relationship. Great success brought with it problems we had never imagined, some of which we were unable to face wisely. No one can prepare you for such events and I lacked the maturity and understanding required. I guess it was easier to stand by each other when we were struggling than when we succeeded, especially to such great heights. In any event, no matter what our problems, Oracene is an amazing force for good in this family, and she remains one of the best women I have ever known in my life.

It is important to remember that faith connects to every element of the Williams Triangle, and connects each element to the others. Chris Evert is a great example when you're talking about faith and confidence. When she was thirteen, I saw the faith she had that she would win. She was one of many people of faith I have seen over the years and it's essential to their victories. Alice Marble, winner of eighteen Grand Slam championships, despite personal tragedies, had so much faith she was able to stand up against the whole world. She championed twenty-three-year-old Althea Gibson when the white establishment refused her entry into the 1950 U.S. Nationals. Marble, who had won the Nationals four times, wrote in the July 1950 issue of *American Lawn Tennis* magazine, "If Althea Gibson represents a challenge to the present crop of women players, it's only fair that they should meet that challenge on the courts." She added, "If tennis is a game for ladies and gentlemen, it's also time we acted a little more like gentle-people and less like sanctimonious hypocrites." If Gibson was not allowed to compete, she concluded, "then there is an ineradicable mark against a game to which I have devoted most of my life, and I would be bitterly ashamed." Due to her stand, Gibson was given entry into the 1950 U.S. Championships, becoming the first African-American player to compete in a Grand Slam event.

Althea Gibson herself went through so much. She could throw a ball as hard as a man, dance better than a man, hit the golf ball better than a man, and struggled against racism all her career, yet she never lost her faith. Faith breeds confidence. Confidence comes from a fundamental belief in spirit and in God. It is vital to success in life, in tennis, in investing, or even in cutting the lawn or whatever you set out to do, big or small. You gain all the confidence in the world when you believe. We sometimes live through trials and tribulations. Life goes wrong from time to time. Faith gives you the confidence to carry on.

I wanted my children to have faith. I believed faith was essential to rearing successful children. Faith and confidence work hand in hand, side by side. If you don't have confidence that you can do something, you're never going to achieve it. It's where the strength to finish the match comes from. The stronger children's faith, the more confident they are, the more attractive they are as friends and models, and the more they exhibit that confidence among their peers and adults.

If you solve things for your children, they cannot learn to have faith in themselves. The only thing they will have faith in is you. They will not have faith in God because their faith has never been tested. It has been stolen. Too many parents interfere with their children and prevent them from taking responsibility for working out their problems. Therefore, the children's faith does not grow. They don't get stronger. They get weaker, more needy, and more dependent.

I saw lots of tennis parents get upset with their children, more so than in any other sport. *She should be doing better. I wish he would take more responsibility. I wish he would practice harder. She could have beaten that girl if she played harder.* Then the parents impose more rules or harsher punishment. More stress. More damage. Where did the responsibility go? They took it away. The young person doesn't have enough experience at trial and error and making mistakes to know what is right or wrong.

Serena told me it was very important to her to feel we had faith in her as she was growing up. She explained it this way: "As we got older, my dad trusted us. He wasn't the kind of parent who told us, 'You have to do this,' or, 'You have to be that.' Even when my mom moved out, we always did what we were supposed to do without being told. Venus had a car at sixteen that she bought herself, and we went to the movies and to practice. We did everything. He trusted us, and we didn't do anything bad, *because* he trusted us. The faith he put in us made us not have to manipulate him. He gave us expectations that we wanted to live up to. That was the way we were raised. When I got my first check at sixteen, and it was a check for a million dollars as a signing bonus, he just gave it to me. Usually, parents take the kid's money away or try and manage it. He just gave it to me and asked me if I was going to be like some athletes and go broke, or was I going to make the right decisions? Now that's faith, and I've always tried to live up to it. I plan to do a lot of the same things when I am a parent."

When Venus played the 1997 U.S. Open, she was interviewed on a major television show right before the final against Martina Hingis. In a conversation with the host, she said, "I don't have to come home now, Daddy, 'cause I'm in the final."

I'd been telling her to come home because she needed to be back in school. "Venus," I said, "I know you're seventeen, but you can't live in my house and not go to school."

Venus did not see it that way. "Daddy, did you see my grades? How I hit the ball?"

"Yeah, I seen all of that, Venus, but my deal with you was until you turned eighteen, you had to be a college student if you livin' in this house."

Now some might say I was contradicting myself. I helped make her a professional tennis player, and I wanted her to be number one, but I also wanted her to have a college education. I was so afraid of what I saw in other young tennis players that sometimes I wished I had never put her in tennis. I had seen parents abuse their children, make bad financial decisions for them, or put them under so much pressure they had emotional breakdowns. I had seen kids come from the best neighborhoods with damaged wrists from too much practice. How painful it is when a kid comes to you and says, "Mr. Williams, does your daughter get a whipping if she loses, like I do?"

I got so worried, it came to a point where I wanted Venus and Serena out of tennis.

Venus said, "Oh, no, I'm not gettin' out of tennis."

There was a magazine in Florida called *Florida Tennis,* and they wanted me to write for them. I wrote three articles. One of them was called "There's a Life Beyond the Baseline." I wrote that if you don't learn there's a life beyond tennis, you will go through life with nothing in your head. During those days, the average education on the women's tour was a junior high school education. I was not going to allow that to happen to my kids. I told Venus that if she didn't go back to school, she couldn't live with me in my house anymore.

Venus decided to buy her own house.

A lot of people predicted she would move a long way away. She had engineers and architects to help her get the house together. She looked all over for a location. She talked about other states. In the end, she bought a huge house about five miles from mine. Then I found out Serena was moving in with her.

I said, "Serena, you only sixteen."

"I'm goin' with Venus," she said flatly, and that's how they both ended up moving out of the house, because I wanted them to be full-time students and they wanted to play professional tennis.

Looking back, I can only feel it was wonderful that they did both, and did them so well. They had faith that their way was right, and the confidence to back it up. They had grown from toddlers to tennis champs and were going forth to live their own lives with faith and courage.

Nothing could please a parent more. However, even I didn't really know what guts they had—until we faced the crowd at a place called Indian Wells.

CHAPTER **TWENTY-TWO**

Wait on the Lord; be of good courage,
and he shall strengthen your heart;
Wait, I say, on the Lord!

PSALM 27:14

Courage is a magnificent thing. It's the strength of heart to triumph we find within us. Courage comes when you do not have the best of everything. It comes when you have the worst of everything. Courage comes when you set your life goal to make something out of nothing. It comes when you are laughed at and belittled but keep on going. Courage comes when you are picked on, but fight back. Courage comes when it seems like everyone has turned against you, and does not understand you, and leaves you standing all alone—and still you go on.

Courage is hope.

Courage is going one more step while the next person falls short. Courage is being able to smile when the whole world is against you. Courage is when you put trust in what's right and come out victorious—and even if you don't, you take heart in the knowledge you let God's will be done, and prayed for your enemies.

I saw true courage on Saturday, March 17, 2001, when the community of Indian Wells, California, disgraced America.

Indian Wells was far from the average community. Compared to Compton, which my family and I had driven from a week earlier, it was different as day and night. Located in Riverside County in the middle of the desert, framed by the beauty of the Santa Rosa Mountains accented in snow, Indian Wells was simply perfect; the perfect sunset, the perfect stadium, the perfect tennis tournament. The grass at Indian Wells was greener than any I'd ever seen before. Palm trees stood like soldiers at attention along perfectly clean streets with lights shining on them bright as diamonds. Flowers blossomed in every direction. Rolls-Royces, Bentleys, Alfa Romeos, Jags, and Mercedeses sat casually in the spotless driveways of exquisite mansions.

In a place like this, a black man had to be on his best behavior.

People who lived in this community did not tolerate foolishness. Unlike Compton, staggering drunks or drug addicts would find no comfort. There were no gangbangers here, no Crips, no Bloods.

We had come here to play the Tennis Master Series tournament. It was going well. The girls were winning, their stars steadily rising. The world seemed perfect. No act of violence could occur here. Open-minded and liberal, the people here could never show racism or prejudice. Unusual for me, I felt welcome, till things suddenly exploded in a way I could never have predicted.

Venus and Serena both won their quarterfinal matches and were due to face each other in the semifinals. It was going to be a closely watched match. Two young female tennis players, sisters, who burst upon the world stage and challenged the white tennis establishment, were going to challenge each other. I always discussed strategy with the girls before a match, but with Venus playing Serena, there was no strategy. Each one would do her best. During practice, my only advice was, "Have fun."

The only cloud on the horizon was that Venus had hurt her knee during her quarterfinal match against Elena Dementieva. We watched her carefully during her practice session. It was increasingly painful. After practice that day, enthusiastic fans surrounded the girls, pleading for autographs. The crowd got so large, Venus and Serena were whisked off by security onto a waiting golf cart and taken to their dressing rooms to prepare for their match, just hours away.

As my daughters continued their success, I had a responsibility as their father to make sure they kept everything in perspective, mentally, emotionally, and physically. That's why injuries were such a dilemma. Thousands of people had paid good money to see Venus and Serena play, and hundreds of tournament organizers had worked for weeks or months and had millions of dollars at stake. How could we disappoint all those people? Yet, I also had a responsibility to Venus herself. If Venus played hurt, she risked permanent injury and, potentially, the end of her career.

That's what we faced, right before the tournament semifinals. Knees are a tennis player's nightmare. With a knee injury, you can't play anywhere near the top of your game. My rule was firm. The girls decided for themselves if an injury required them to withdraw. They knew their bodies best. Venus was really in pain. Three doctors examined her before the match, and while she made it clear she keenly wanted to play against her sister, they advised her not to do so. The doctors were not concerned about the fans, the sponsors, or the television network. Their only concern was Venus's physical ability to perform without causing more injury.

Venus notified the tournament trainer that she had to withdraw. I believed she made a mature and good decision. We did everything by the WTA book, but the tournament officials didn't want Venus to pull out so they kept stalling. They waited till just five minutes before the match was scheduled to go on before they finally announced that Venus couldn't play. It got nasty almost at once. Now, if Venus said she couldn't play, she couldn't play. Both Serena and I knew that without doubt. But suddenly we, and especially me, were accused of everything from fixing the match to manipulating the rankings. It was all foolishness, but when we were interviewed after the cancellation, the antagonism of broadcasters was palpable.

The fans' anger simmered like a volcano through the following day, and by the time we arrived to play the finals, the eruption was inevitable. The heat of it fell on Serena, Venus, and me. When Venus and I entered the stadium, we were booed steadily. The media speculated about why the crowd booed, but to my knowledge, not one spectator was ever interviewed. Paying customers have every right to voice their opinion at a sporting event, but tennis etiquette has always been required. Why was such rude behavior so uniformly defended?

The chorus of boos that cascaded through the stadium sent a powerful message to America, to Venus, to Serena, and to me. It was a message from the past, one America tries to put behind it but can never forget. It was a snapshot from the days when the open humiliation of the black race was accepted without question. Accusations and racial epithets flew through the stadium. No one questioned the unruly behavior of the fans. The only thing in question was our character and integrity. My daughters were treated without an ounce of dignity or respect. They were treated like criminals. How Serena managed to come out to play, and how Venus managed to keep her composure without breaking down, can only be credited to their spiritual strength and the training they received as children on the courts of Compton.

Deep down inside, I kept asking for a higher power to lead and guide us as we sustained the verbal lashing. My mom had always taught me, when white people did or said something I did not approve of, to hold my head up high and ignore them. I never liked doing it then, and didn't do it often or well, but that was exactly what I did that day.

I did not know that events at Indian Wells were destined to follow me wherever I went. From radio stations in Los Angeles, to newspapers in New York, to television stations throughout the world, the talk was about Richard Williams and his tennis-playing daughters. The media called me a racist and the tennis father from hell. They said I was manipulating the powerful tennis industry and I needed to be silenced.

He's destroying his daughters marketing and advertising abilities, they cried.

Venus and Serena need a new coach. Richard is in the way.

Why doesn't he just let them play?

I tried to respond. It turned out I was damned if I did, damned if I didn't. The powerful mass media that disseminate information at the speed of light were relentless. The following is an excerpt from a *Los Angeles Times* column by Bill Dwyre, reprinted in "What Happened at Indian Wells?" by Joel Drucker, published on ESPN.com on March 11, 2009.

If these situations are truly just happenstance; if Venus's knee truly did get sore just in time for her match with Serena; if all this is just the product of a bunch of jealous competitors on the women's tour and a bunch of dopes with overactive curiosity glands, then why don't the Williamses set the record straight? When they are asked about the rumor and innuendo that constantly swirl around them, they respond with smirks and half-hearted denials. They deny, but with less than the normal conviction, even anger, one would expect in the face of such serious issues. How about pounding on the table and saying it ain't so? How about some tears, some anger?

Would another family have been treated as mine was? The answer to me is obvious. America offers dreams and nightmares, ease and struggle, trial and tribulation. The harsh reality is that it has not eradicated prejudice. Racial barriers have fallen in record numbers throughout the years. Blacks not only ride in the front of the bus, some of us own the bus company. The events at Indian Wells were a reminder of how much farther we had to go. Venus and I sat in that stadium subjected to painful boos and jeers. I was called "nigger." Each time the word reached my ears, I closed my fist tighter till the bones in my hands ached. I was fifty-nine years old at that time, and I had allowed myself to believe things had changed. This was a sign that things had gotten worse. I tried to reason with myself and not allow someone else's stupidity to reinforce my own. I struggled to keep my mouth closed because I was eager to lay a holy cursing on someone.

"Relax," I whispered to myself over and over, "stay calm."

A white man sitting in the second row yelled out, "Nigger, if this was back in '65, I'd skin your black ass alive."

I looked him straight in the eye and said, "Why don't you act like it's '65?"

I actually made a move in his direction but he scampered

away when another man said to him, "Leave those niggers alone, and just boo the hell out of them."

The sound of the angry crowd filled my head with voices from every direction of the stadium.

We don't need a nigger in charge of tennis.

Let's boo that nigger the whole match.

He wants to be called Mr. Williams but I call him Mr. Nigger.

We don't want niggers out here anyway.

If you don't like it, play your own tournament.

That's why all the tennis players hate you now.

The words stung. Hot beads of perspiration poured down my face. I was devastated. The year was 2001. How could the same racial issues I confronted in 1950 reach across time and imperil my daughters? I was told that prejudice did not exist in professional tennis. That proved to be untrue. What I found out was that prejudice did exist. It was accompanied by hate.

As Serena walked into the almost-filled-to-capacity stadium, she was met with an onslaught of boos. Did they realize they were insulting an American champion who had won the U.S. Open and successfully represented her country in the 2000 Olympics? Only hate would compel people to turn their backs on her that way.

The crowd booed Serena as she got ready to play Kim Clijsters for the championship. People applauded her double faults and unforced errors. Blacks have long been accustomed to being belittled, criticized, and treated like second-class citizens. Here was proof that race still played a role in sports as Serena experienced firsthand the results of hate. Being black in a traditionally white sport, we had often been met with criticism and condemnation. We used to say, "You can dress a black man up, but in the eyes of a white man he's still just a dressed-up nigger." We had put a black tennis player on the podium of Olympic victory, but when she came down, she was still just another nigger.

According to one of the commentators, "The fans are looking for someone to blame for the situation. They [Serena and Venus] really shouldn't be in the same tournament. It's not fair for everybody to be left wondering."

Fair?

Did he mean it was fair for thousands of fans to jeer a teenager because they believed the accusations against me for fixing games when both Venus and Serena played the same tournament? Even Elena Dementieva, when she was asked at her news conference after losing the quarterfinal to Venus, "Any predictions on tomorrow's match between sisters?" answered, "I mean, I don't know what Richard thinks about it. I think he will decide who's going to win tomorrow."

Here was the truth of that day. A doctor confirmed Venus's injury and instructed her not to play. That decision was met with suspicion and distrust because we were not white.

The reception we received that day at the Master Series final at Indian Wells was heartbreaking, but Serena rose to meet the challenge with real courage. She prayed for the strength to endure and refused to quit even when it felt like the whole world was against her.

Later, she told me, "I went over on the changeover and I prayed to God just to help me be strong, not even to win, but to be strong, not to listen to the crowd. I just wanted some strength to go on."

The difference between an ordinary person and an extraordinary person is simple. The extraordinary person is willing to fight a little harder. Serena proved no matter how harsh the treatment, she had the faith to overcome, the strength to make a stand, and the courage to keep fighting.

When the last ball was hit, Serena held her hands up in victory. The audience had a mixed reaction. Some booed, some applauded. When Serena came over to hug Venus and me, the boos echoed through the stadium. I will remember that moment as long as I live. Commentators made excuses for the audience. They were just as guilty. One announcer said I requested a security guard. That was a lie. At no time did I request security. I believe the guard's presence was a way of adding fuel to the fire by whoever sent him.

The memory of Indian Wells will always leave a sour taste in my mouth, but I want this statement to stand beside it. It would be a grave injustice to allow people to believe that every single individual in the stadium was against us. In the midst of the jeering, I could hear the voices of some who cheered for us. For them, I leave this message. What better friend than a friend who is willing to stand up for you in a time of trouble, in your time of need, when the whole world has turned its back on you? Regardless of how many people jeered us and called me nigger, today I still believe I had friends at Indian Wells. Thank you.

That day, Serena was a true champion. She let no one else define her or her family, not with insults or with accusations. She rose to victory and defined herself. When she won the match, she faced the crowd from the center of the stadium court and said, "First and foremost, I'd like to thank my God, Jehovah, because you guys were a little tough on me today. I'd like to thank my dad, my family, my sister, and the sponsors. And I'd like to thank Kim for providing such a wonderful final. I'd like to thank everyone who supported me, and if you didn't, I love you guys anyway."

That is the courage of a true champion.

CHAPTER **TWENTY-THREE**

For I know the plans I have for you,
declares the Lord, plans to prosper
you and not to harm you, plans to
give you hope and a future.

JEREMIAH 29:11

I am a great planner. It's the way I approach life. My plan to
teach Venus and Serena to play tennis began with the seventy-
eight-page written document I created before they were even
born. I had a goal. I needed a plan to pursue it. The reality of
our situation was that we had no shot at winning. We lived in
the ghetto. We had no tennis background. The decision to raise
the best tennis players in the world required planning that was
outside the bounds of our family experience. We knew very
few people in what was, and still is, an overwhelmingly white
sport. We had no way to begin—except to pick up our secondhand racquets and balls and begin to play.

Along the way, we learned a great deal. Not all of it was
about tennis. The greatest learning was about life. One of the

reasons I wrote this book was to share that experience with you. If you want to raise kids to be champions at life, sports, academics, or anything else, I've put together the most important principles I gathered as a father, a teacher, and a man. These principles are the result of a lifetime of learning, and putting into practice what I learned. I call them my Top Ten Rules for Success.

Top Ten Rules for Success

1. Failing to plan is planning to fail.
2. Always be positive.
3. Confidence is essential to success.
4. Faith is essential to confidence.
5. When you fail, you fail alone.
6. You learn by looking, seeing, and listening.
7. Create theories and test them out.
8. Always have a Plan B.
9. An appreciative child is a blessing.
10. Let no one define you but you.

I can't say I had these rules so neatly put together in the beginning, but over the years, as our successes mounted, I came to realize these were the ideas that mattered most. First, I believe that failing to plan is planning to fail. Planning is not faith. It's not an accident. It's the deliberate attempt to succeed. A child should be taught not only how to plan, but how to *write* a plan. Writing clarifies thinking. It defines the actions we are going to take to achieve our plan.

I want to be honest. I wanted my kids to be the best tennis players in the world because I didn't have faith that *I* could make millions of dollars. I wanted them to have that level of success, and I didn't believe I could give it to them on my own.

Over the years, I asked a lot of parents, "Why did *you* put your child into tennis?"

The usual reply is, "Oh, they love it so much."

I've never seen one child love tennis so much that they'd give up everything for it, including their free time. They might like to hit the ball, and tennis is a great family sport, but when you're talking about putting children out there by themselves for hours every day, for years, no child really wants that. To teach my kids to follow the plan, I asked them how many dollars they would like to earn. Then I wrote down top incomes from many jobs and professions. I asked them which income they would prefer to have. They picked sports every time.

Most parents don't teach their kids to plan because they don't know how to plan themselves. Here's where you have to create theories and test them out. I may believe X or Y, but is X or Y working? Are we closer to the goal we have set? Should this action be maintained? Is this person successful enough for me to listen to? Don't do what others say is the "best" for your children, if they are not where you want them to be. If what you try doesn't work, have a Plan B ready. If tennis failed, my Plan B was education. It was a perfect Plan B because either way, they would be prepared for the world they would have to face.

I read somewhere that Serena said she never liked tennis. At such an early age, who would? At three and four years old, she and her sister were on the court hitting tennis balls while other girls were going to Chuck E. Cheese to eat, have fun, and ride the slides. Knowing that, I tried my best not to make them bored. We never practiced like at the big tennis academies. I tried to make it fun and I never criticized them, no matter what they did. And we were always at their side, Oracene and

I, working together, teaching together, melding our different styles to bring the best out in both of them.

How do you get a child to be great? You make them think great. I believe whatever you put in a child's mind will last forever, whether you want it to or not. For that reason, I would always tell them they were great. Once Venus hit a ball so badly, it went way over the fence. Nobody could hit a ball that bad. But how did I know what she was trying to do? She could have been experimenting. It didn't matter. To me, every shot was a good shot.

I said, "Great shot."

She stopped, looked at me, and said, "Do you really believe that's a great shot?"

I said, "Oh, yeah, you can't be beat, hitting it like that. Great shot, Venus."

She just laughed.

What happened years in the future? Venus was playing the Australian Open, a Grand Slam tournament. You only have four Grand Slams all year. In one game, she hit a serve so wrong it went way up in the stands. Like the second deck. It went so far up that Venus had to cup her hands over her eyes to find it. For other players, it could have been an embarrassing moment that broke their concentration. Not Venus. When she finally saw where it landed, the first thing she did was laugh. She didn't put any pressure on herself because she wasn't ever taught pressure. She thought that serve was great because she had been taught greatness all her life.

From the time the girls were tiny, whatever they did, I said, "That's great." Venus was three, and we were in the park, and she had to go pee-pee, so she did, right there. Her mom started yelling but I said, "Let her. Don't yell or slap her. Let her pee-pee," and I told Venus she was great. I meant it. Everything the kids did, it was great. They would put on their own shows at home, I told them they were great. They'd bring home their grades, I'd say, "Your grade is great." Now, their grades were great because they didn't have any choice. I told them, "You're great—so you can't bring in nothin' but A-pluses here." That was what was expected. They were taught if you can't bring in an A-plus, it's your fault. Don't you go blaming the teacher or the school. It's *your* responsibility.

Good manners are a responsibility, too. No parent should ever let praise be an excuse to accept bad manners. Serena put it very simply when she was asked about her home. "Let me be honest with you. In a black family, you don't get angry, you don't talk back, and you don't yell, because that's not allowed. I don't know what they show you on TV, but it's not allowed in black families. You do what you're told or you learn a lesson. You don't talk back or disrespect your parents."

We never had trouble with manners in any of our kids, and to this day, I believe my daughters are some of the most well-mannered people in the world. They have been that way since they were children. A well-mannered child is a great asset to a family and will have a much easier time succeeding in the world.

Always be positive. I tried always to be positive. I don't know if I always succeeded, but I sure tried my best to be positive every day. That way, I planted hope in their minds. It was the same with Serena as it was with Venus. One time when Serena blasted the ball into the net time after time, and it seemed as if her control had just about deserted her, I just smiled and said the harshest thing I think I ever said to her on the court, "Serena, it seems like the ball has a mind of its own today."

Once practice or a tournament was over, it was over. Tennis was not life. Venus had a problem in this area. When she first played junior tournaments, she loved to win. She won a lot, too, but once it was over, I couldn't stop her from talking about it. On the way home, I told her, "Venus, I don't want to talk about the tournament. We could talk about education or books or homework, but tennis and winning is over for now."

Still, she couldn't stop talking about the match, so I stopped at a store and said, "Venus, would you like to have something to drink?"

"Yes, Daddy."

"Go in and get something to drink, then."

She was so happy when she went in the store. I kept driving. When I got home, her mother said to me, "Where's Venus?"

I said, "The last time I saw her she was going into the store for a drink."

"Didn't you wait for her?"

"No."

"You didn't go in with her?"

"No. She talked about tennis too doggone much for me."

Oracene left immediately to get Venus, but from that day on it was rare that Venus, Serena, or I talked about tennis after the match was over. If you lost, you lost. If you won, you won. I didn't want to dissect it. I see parents complaining when their children come off the court after losing a match. It's disgraceful. Those girls or boys fought so hard, so long, they deserve only love and praise. Instead, they get disgust. That is the worst emotion a parent can ever give to a child. If my girls won, they had done the best they could. If they lost, they had done the best they could. Sadly, it isn't always that way with others. I've seen everything bad out there. I saw matches in Southern California so serious that the boys would fight on the court and Jim

Hillman, retired now from the Southern California Tennis Association, had to run out to stop them.

At one junior tournament, I was in a hurry to bring Venus somewhere, but I knew she would easily have her match over in thirty minutes. Forty minutes passed. Fifty minutes passed. I went to see what was wrong. As I watched, every time Venus hit a winner, the girl called it out. Venus didn't mind staying all day, but I did. I took the other player's father aside and told him, "Look, man, I don't mind you and your daughter cheating, but today I have to go. Why don't you tell her to start calling the balls right?"

He refused, and I actually had to take him out back and threaten him to get him to tell his daughter to call the match fairly. What had he taught her? She had to win at all costs. Honor and integrity meant nothing. With that kind of parental attitude, I could only imagine the beating the girl was going to get when she got home after losing the match to Venus.

Most parents who go into athletics with their kids have great intentions. They spend a ton of money and work unbelievable hours, hitting, traveling, supporting, and teaching. But some parents become so invested, they become angry if they don't see progress and take it out on the child. Parents have to be very careful. You can't make someone develop against his or her schedule. I couldn't get Serena to catch up with Venus or Venus to do what it took to catch Serena. Children learn in their own time, and if they're going to be good, they're going to be good almost despite anything you can do.

Then there are the parents who think that what they need is to get their child a John McEnroe racquet, or something like it. What they don't realize is McEnroe had a great gift. He was so gifted there's not another like him. I heard McEnroe once say that he didn't like all the training. I don't care what you do or how you do it. If your child is going to be good, he or she will be good anyway. The advice I give to parents is to let your children develop their own schedule, their own style, and be as patient as you can. If you can't be patient, take your child to practice and just stay away until it's over.

My problem was, by the time Venus and Serena were ready to start playing tournaments, they had developed too much too soon. When Venus was ten, we went to a tournament, but when we got there, she had to play up to the twelves. She beat the twelve-year-old so easily it was unbelievable. We went to another league and she played in the sixteen-year-old division and beat up those girls, too. It was then I realized she was way too far ahead of schedule for what I wanted her to be.

Too many kids lose their childhood playing professional sports, especially tennis. First and foremost, I wanted her to be a child. You can't be an adult without having a childhood. That's why so many athletes grow up and act like children. They spend their money like children. They get on drugs like children. They break the law like children. They berate other people like spoiled children. It's all they know.

Mom used to say that "family life is a major university by itself." She was right. My theory is if you allow a child to be a child, and train like a child, and be treated like a child, that child will grow up to be a great adult. For that reason, and I really got criticized for it, I cut back a hell of a lot. It was very hard to hold Venus back when she was twelve years old because she was ready to play professional tennis. When she was fourteen, she was ready to take over her career, but I couldn't allow that. The first match she ever played, she played a girl name Shawn. Venus beat her so easily, it looked like she could beat nearly anyone in the world. I knew then that Venus shouldn't play another tournament that year. Not one. If, at fourteen, she could beat a player ranked in the top one hundred in the world, and beat her so easily, maybe she could beat the world number thirty or forty player. She was just too far ahead of schedule. I had to hold her. Winning would take away her childhood. Suddenly, she'd be grown. Everybody would want to get her into this tournament or that. Let's give her a wild card—and I'd lose control of my daughter's right to be a child.

The next match Venus played was against the fine Spanish player Arantxa Sánchez Vicario, the one who later on, sadly, lost all her money. Then, she was number two in the world. Venus took the first set from her easily. Although Venus eventually lost the match, Arantxa had to struggle to beat her. Afterward, I said, "Venus is too far ahead. Why don't we take her to Magic Mountain or Knott's Berry Farm for a vacation?"

Parents must always remember it takes years to be an adult. In 1990, at sixteen, Monica Seles was the youngest-ever French Open champion, and world number one. Venus started thinking if Monica Seles could do it, *she* could do it. I told her, you live in this house, you're going to go to school. The fact that Monica was sixteen didn't mean she belonged there. At that age, even the law looks at you as a child. It was hard for someone with Venus's drive and talent to accept that, but adults have to be in charge. I made her a promise that the day that she turned eighteen, she could go for it all, but until then, she'd abide by the house rules. The house rules were she could play two or three tournaments at sixteen, no more. Nothing was to be gained by playing more than that.

The USTA might not have liked it. The media might not have liked it. People said I was ruining their chances, but how can it ruin children to let them be children? You can never come back in your life and be a child again and you don't ever want to miss it. We've all seen girls and boys out there that didn't have a chance to be a child. Jennifer Capriati had no chance to be a child. She was too good too young, and pushed too far too fast. Both Venus and Serena have thanked me many times for letting them be children. They didn't miss a thing.

Even though tennis was my dream, even though I knew the money would be there, big money, I knew I was going to lose my children if I let them play the way the USTA wanted. Now, which one was more important to me? I looked at cute little Venus and Serena out there. No matter what I did, they were going to love me. No matter how much I fussed at them, they were going to love me—and that was a responsibility I could not betray.

You should never take love and sell it, but some parents do just that. I knew a little girl named Serena, before my own Serena was born. She didn't play tennis. Her mom wanted money so she had victimized her and put her to work out on the street doing bad things. I knew them because I had a security contract at a store near where she was doing drugs and going from bad to worse.

When I tried to explain how her mom was using her, she would say to me, "My mom wouldn't do that to me, would she?"

I hated to tell her the truth because she loved her mom so much, but it was true. It was a shame. That girl is who Serena is named after. I wanted her name to remind me always to value my daughter, always to respect and love her, and put her welfare first.

Choosing between having a child whom you love and who loves you, and money, was easy. I found it even made it easier for me to accept my kids on the court. So many times it went like this:

I don't wanna practice, Daddy.

What you wanna do?

I wanna go shopping.

Let's go!

Every time they asked to come off the court, we went. I saw parents tell their kids they were going to "stay on this damn court till you get it right!" Not me. Not ever. I never was a super coach, but I sure have been, I hope, a super parent.

As we climbed the tennis ladder, we remained a family first and foremost. After practice, the girls worked at their education, went to dance lessons, and did what kids do. Playing only two or three tournaments a year let them work at what they liked. Go on down to the beach, surf, read, whatever. My plan was to make it as much fun as possible—and as uplifting. When the girls got older, we played in different parks, and sometimes at tennis clubs. Sometimes, we'd just go on road trips—anything to be together as a family. I'd rev up our old Volkswagen bus and get everyone inside it and off we'd go.

As Venus and Serena began to have a reputation, I took them to better neighborhoods where homes cost a million dollars. See, girls? You can have that, if you work hard. It's one of my most important rules—you learn a lot by looking, seeing, and listening. I saw they played better in the better neighborhoods. They saw the rewards. They saw the better life. It didn't take a genius to make the connection. They played better there because they could "see" the position they could be in one day. Visual messages sink in. We see them every day and don't even realize it. It's why advertising is so powerful. It's why companies spend fortunes on billboards every year. Later, when we moved to our place in Florida, I put signs up all over our property so they could always learn by looking and seeing. (See the first photo insert.)

For the same reason, I never wanted to criticize my children. Harsh words leave a lasting impression, a negative message. I saw too many fathers who just criticized and never taught anything. It takes a strong child to survive that. I always tried to be positive and give the girls loving messages of strength. Venus was easy. She was as calm as they come, our family child. If the key to success is how well you listen, Venus was always the greatest listener in the house. I never met a child like her, so understanding, so insightful, and so smart. I used to wonder sometimes how she learned all the things she learned.

I put up signs to let Venus know she had the knowledge to make her dreams come true. (See the first photo insert.)

Serena always had power and drive and already knew a lot from watching Venus. It sounds funny, but she was probably way ahead of where I thought she was, at a very early age. We still laugh when she tells the story of her first tournament when she was eight.

"My dad only let Venus play because she could beat him in singles. I got angry and told him I felt I should play, too. In the Volkswagen bus, he told me, 'If you can beat me, then I'll let you play this tournament.' Now, Venus had waited a really long time, and had lost. She was mad at him until they played again and she won. I was really happy for her, but I couldn't beat my dad, so I figured out a way around it. Like he says, Venus is all about honesty and truth, but he doesn't say that about me because, if the truth be told, I'm about schemes. When I saw two application forms on my dad's desk at home, obviously one for Venus, I filled out the other one for myself and sent it in. On the day of the tournament, while Venus was playing, I just went up to the registration table and took my place in the other side of the draw."

Can you believe that? I'm smiling as I think about it, but there I was, having told Serena to go off and play on the swings or something, while I went to watch Venus. A few hours later, people were coming over to me saying, "Hey, did you know your daughter is winning?"

I said, "Sure, I can see that."

"No, Mr. Williams, we mean Serena."

I couldn't figure out what kind of game Serena was playing on the swings that it was so important that she was winning it. That's when I found out that she had entered herself in the match. When she won, I was very proud. Both of my daughters were winners that day. I was so pleased at Serena's success, I wasn't going to do anything but praise her. However, I put up a sign that read, "Serena, you must learn to listen." (See the first photo insert.)

I learned a lot by watching and listening, too. No one can predict everything. No one knows everything. If we fail to learn, we fail to change. No matter how hard I stuck to my plan, I was always willing to modify it in the light of experience. I saw that neither Venus nor Serena had the same enthusiasm when we worked out in Compton as when we went to fancy places like the Riviera Country Club in Pacific Palisades, so I allowed them to play there. It had a surprising impact on all of us.

When Venus was nine years old, we were at Riviera for a junior tournament. The girls had finished their practice and I was off looking at the buildings and marveling at how well they kept the grounds and the courts. When I got back,

I found Venus and Serena sitting happily at the pool like two little princesses, each with a hamburger, French fries, and a big milk shake.

"How did you get these?" I asked, surprised because I knew they didn't have any money.

Serena grinned. "It's on my tab."

I sat there for about two minutes, thinking about how to correct *that* attitude. We were Compton, not country club, right?

"Would you girls like to live here?" I asked.

They looked at me like I was crazy.

"No? Then you can get out and walk yourselves right on back to the car," I said, "because you know where you live at, and you're not allowed to live that way. I brought you peanut butter and jelly sandwiches and that's what you have to eat. Don't let me ever see this *'It's on my tab'* no more."

You learn a lot by listening, seeing, and looking. Well, me, too. I saw the look on their faces as they followed me to the car. They didn't get it. They were only kids. They had been told the meal was free and I wasn't there to tell them different. This time, it was my turn to learn a lesson.

"Hold on, kids. Go back and eat what you ordered and enjoy it," I told them, and they scampered off happily.

When I first saw Venus and Serena eating that way, I was upset. No eating ice cream, hamburgers, and French fries. It's not our style. But they were just kids. I was being unreasonable expecting them to know what I had not taught them. So when you plan, remember that you're planning for children. A child doesn't think like an adult. That day I learned it's easy, being an adult, to think as an adult, to act as an adult, and make decisions as an adult. I had all my nice adult plans. I just forgot to remember they were for children.

It's a great thing when children have their own plans and

share them with their parents or adults. I learned a lot letting my kids teach me. Most kids do not want to announce they don't know something. As often as not, they will not share with you what they do not understand. But you can always come to a subject on a child's level and act like you don't know it. I had to do that a lot of times.

"I don't understand that new math, Serena. I can't help you."

"I'll show you, Daddy. This is the way," and she went to the teacher to get the information to teach me.

I found that I had a better relationship that way, by not knowing too damn much. It allowed them to feel intelligent and useful. It was another thing I learned from wanting to be the best father I could be.

I didn't have a real father to learn from, so I read books and talked to different people, and spent my time thinking up neat things to do, and fun ways for them to learn. There are many things that help you be a better parent. Work together as a family, but be spontaneous together as well. No planning, just be happy together, and laugh. I believe that every day God provides a way for us to learn something of value and to teach our children the same. One time, I took everyone on a family outing. It was a great idea, but we ran into many problems. My old Volkswagen bus could fit the five girls and me and Oracene inside. It was always fun. We'd go for a ride and have dinner out somewhere, an early dinner, probably the earliest dinner anyone ate, often around 3:30 p.m. so we could keep riding.

Another of my rules is that when you succeed, everyone is there, but when you fail, you fail alone. This is why you always want to succeed. This trip proved it. The Volkswagen's clutch broke in San Jose, California, four hundred miles from home, and all I had was fifty dollars in my pocket. Where were we going to get the car fixed, and eat and spend the night, five kids and two adults, on fifty bucks?

I'm hungry, Daddy.

I'm hungry, too, Daddy.

Me, too, Daddy.

It went on. I had no credit cards. No checkbook. I didn't take anything because we were just going driving and I never intended to go so far from home. It had to be me to the rescue. I got some pliers and a wire coat hanger, crawled under the car, and bent the hanger to secure the clutch. It looked perfect. To the cheers of all, I drove us off—and got ten yards before the coat hanger broke, the clutch blew out, and the car stopped dead.

There I was, standing with the family and the dead car on the side of the road with everyone commenting not so kindly on my mechanical ability, when a gentleman in a tow truck saw us and pulled over. He got out and walked over. We had gotten some recognition for how the girls were playing, but it was still new to me when I saw it on his face.

"Excuse me," he said, "are you Richard Williams?"

"Yes, sir. I am."

"Mr. Williams, I've heard about you and your girls."

"You have?"

He nodded and pointed to the car. "You have a problem?"

"We sure do," I agreed. "My clutch is shot. We live way down in Compton and I never intended to come this far. I only brought fifty dollars."

He thought for a minute. "Tell you what," he said. "I can tow your car to the station, but I can't get a clutch cable until tomorrow because we don't have foreign cars there. I have to drive to San Francisco or Oakland to get it."

"That sounds fine to me," I said, trying to figure out how we were all going to sleep in the car. The girls might have been thinking the same thing because none of their faces looked very happy.

"And for tonight," the man continued, "I'll put you guys up in a motel and when you get home you can send the money back to me."

All of a sudden, there were smiles everywhere. Cheers, almost. The kids thought this was just great because they would get to stay in a motel. The whole outing turned into a great trip. I had failed alone, but I had succeeded in front of everyone.

Early the next morning, we got a clutch cable and he fixed the bus. I thanked him and drove home. I lost no time. I went right to the bank and picked up the money I owed him, but instead of mailing it, I got everyone back in the car and we drove all the way back to give it to him personally.

When we got there, he said, "You didn't have to come back, Mr. Williams. I knew you were good for it. You could've mailed it to me."

That was true enough, but I didn't think it showed the proper appreciation. It wouldn't show how much we owed this man for what he did for us. That was the lesson I wanted to teach the children. It was a very important one. When you're raising your children, one of the greatest things you can teach them is to appreciate what they get from the home they live in. Ninety-nine percent of the time, if they're not taught that, they will think what they receive is automatic. They automatically get food. They automatically get clothes. They automatically get a two-seater car. I found that once my children learned to appreciate what they received, they accepted the plans I had for them without griping or complaining. Appreciating what they got was almost more important than anything we gave them. They learned to appreciate their family. They learned to appreciate being women. They learned to appreciate their talent. It was easier for me to plan with them. I even enjoyed it more because they'd say, "Oh, thank you, Dad, for gettin' this for me."

I could always tell when their mom took them out to eat because they showed their appreciation when they came home. "You know what, Dad? I brought you a little of my cake," or, "I brought you a little piece of this here."

Their appreciation made me superproud to be a dad. It was a great lesson for me. I didn't know how important appreciation was when I wrote my plan originally. What a great thing it was for me to learn. I went back to my plan and added, "Teach appreciation," and added all kinds of thoughts on it. That lesson remains one of my most valuable discoveries as a parent. An appreciative child is a blessing beyond measure, and a joy to the world.

Amen.

CHAPTER **TWENTY-FOUR**

In the day when I cried, thou
answered me, and strengthened
me with strength in my soul.
PSALM 138:3

The loss of a child is every parent's nightmare. Our daughter, Yetunde Price, was thirty-one years old, the eldest of our five children and mother to three children of her own, when she was murdered on the streets of Compton in 2003. She was shot in the head by a Crips gang member while riding in a car driven by her boyfriend.

Yetunde was a great daughter who would have done great things in her life had she been able to live it. Her death was a major blow to us. Yetunde was a unique individual. When she wanted to do something, she'd stand behind me and say in her nice, sweet, lovely little way, "Daddy, may I please do this? May I please do that?"

I couldn't help but say yes.

Yetunde was just a terrific human being, easy to understand, ambitious, and always involved with the family. She helped manage Venus and Serena. She knew how to give her opinion and take care of things when Venus and Serena turned professional. Yetunde paid bills, made sure the insurance on the cars was always up to date, and was always a major help. Yet, she wanted to live her own life and pursue her own dreams. When I moved the family to Florida, Yetunde decided not to come. She wanted to stay in California and, bless her soul, that's where she's buried.

After all the time we spent in Compton, and all the contact I had with the gangs, I ended up having strong relationships within them. Once our enemies, they became our protectors and even guarded Venus and Serena on the very courts from which they had once tried to eject us. I became a father figure of sorts to some, and tried my best to get them out of the gang life. I was rarely successful, but it created some honest dialogue. When I went to California after the shooting, I didn't go directly to see Yetunde's body. I went to see the gang leaders because I wanted to know exactly what had happened.

They said Yetunde's shooting was a mistake. "Mr. Williams, we sorry. We didn't mean to shoot your daughter."

They shared with me what had happened. I came to believe what they told me was true. She was shot by accident. They were after the guy she was with. The killers thought she was driving the car so they shot through the passenger side. The bullet went in the back of her head and out the front. Her face was shattered.

When we gathered in California, I said to her mother, "I don't think you want to see your daughter right now."

"Oh, yes, I do. I want to see my daughter," she insisted.

It was devastating. She got so weak she almost fainted.

Of all the children, I think Serena was the one most bothered by Yetunde's death. I was in Atlanta, Georgia, in the car, when she called me. I could tell by her voice that something major was wrong. She had never sounded like that before.

I said, "Serena, whatever it is that's wrong, please don't tell me. I'm driving the car and I'm in Georgia. Let me get turned around."

I have a thing about death. If it happens, it's over. There is nothing more to be done. Once, in the early days of the girls' success, before we had the kind of security necessary to protect us, the phone rang and some vicious fool told Oracene that Venus and Serena were dead. They had been killed in a car crash. Of course, Oracene tried frantically to get in touch with them. I went to my desk and began to work. If it was true, there was nothing to be done.

I was headed back to my hotel after Serena's call when I heard on the news that Yetunde had been killed. I wanted to call Serena back, but I did not. I just drove, visualizing Yetunde and feeling the pain. It's a terrible thing to lose a child. No one can understand what you go through unless he or she has been through it. There are a lot of groups out there to help parents who lose a child. I never went. I went to my family and we all just talked together and cried together and did the best we could. It was a tough time. We hoped we had done the best job possible for Yetunde. It would have been so easy to start questioning what we had done. Why was she with this person? Why was she in that atmosphere? What could we have done that would have prevented this?

The citizens of Compton brought little dolls and stuffed animals and a cross to the site where Yetunde died. I picked them all up and brought them home. They brought so much sorrow to me that I took the cross and the dolls and the stuffed animals and burnt them all. I couldn't stand the constant reminders of the sadness. I couldn't bear so many people telling me, "I'm so sorry for you." For a long time, I told people, "Whatever you do, don't bring up my daughter's name or anything about her being killed."

Parents reach a point in life where nothing can really hurt us, except through our children. I could live with all that had happened to me, all the beatings, all the pain of growing up in a racist America. I could handle waking up in the middle of the night with all the angry memories in my head. But I could do nothing to stop this pain.

I remember Serena won one tennis tournament and said, "This is for Yetunde." Venus would also always talk about how wonderful she was. They had the same type of love for Yetunde that they had for each other. Yetunde had a way of bringing the family members closer and making our lives better. She could express herself so uniquely that we all felt that we were the closest one to her.

The *New York Times* sent a reporter to cover the trial of the gang member accused of the shooting. He was very nice to me. He went to court all the time, sat through all the trials. After two mistrials, the accused killer pleaded "no contest" and was sent to jail.

After the sentencing, the reporter called me. "Mr. Williams, what do you think? Do you think it's okay?"

I couldn't say I believed the guy sentenced wasn't the guy who did it. The gang was very sure of that and they told me so. They delivered someone who was going to pay. The police accepted it. The courts accepted it. Whatever had been done, it was over. If the guy went to jail or the electric chair, it wasn't going to change a thing.

For me, it was over. I had no more pain left. I had no more animosity. It was over and it was done. Yetunde's life had been fulfilled, no matter how young she was. She was with God now and I could live with that because I had to, despite the pain.

For whatsoever is born of God
overcometh the world: and this
is the victory that overcometh the
world, our faith.

1 John 5:4

CHAPTER **TWENTY-FIVE**

The roar of the crowd at Wimbledon Stadium as Serena won the finals match pulled me back from my thoughts of the past. The cheers pulled me back from Shreveport, back from the cotton fields where my mother toiled in near slavery, back from the fear and danger I had lived with every day as a child. It pulled me back seventy years. I was standing at the end of my journey. What is it like when your plans succeed? There is pride beyond measure. Could I count my blessings? There were so many, I was almost overcome. Watching Serena receive the winner's trophy, tears coursed freely down my cheeks and I didn't care who saw them.

Being a champion starts with a dream, and the dedication and commitment to make that dream come true. A champion is a dream catcher. She catches her dream by any means necessary and follows it through. There are people who will support and believe in her. There are people who will discourage and criticize her. Either way, she has the strength to sustain her battle.

A champion is a true warrior, one so driven by determination that she will stop at nothing to make it to the top. I had seen my daughters' eyes fill with fury as they eyed opponents, anticipating war. A champion is confident she will be the victor. She is completely focused on the prize, and no matter how tough the challenge, she will rise to it. She rises to every occasion with the grace and poise of a queen.

What had I taught my children? That a true champion treasures her unique gift, whatever it is that has been bestowed upon her by God. She treasures her hard work and sacrifice. A champion does not understand the concept of being mediocre or second best. She treasures life and lives it abundantly, to the fullest, aware that life is a precious gift and victory is sweet beyond measure.

Had I succeeded? Had I made up for my father's lack of love and protection for me by loving and protecting my own family? I hoped so. Had I justified all the work and effort in the plan I wrote so many years ago? Three generations told me I had. When Serena sprinted up to the family box and I held her in my arms, I could feel the powerful current of strength and purpose and dignity that flowed from my beloved mother, through my dedicated former wife, to my amazing daughters.

"I thank Jehovah for letting me get this far," Serena said as she held the winner's trophy high. "I almost didn't make it. A few years ago, you know I was in the hospital. But now I'm here again and it's so worth it and I'm so happy. I never dreamt of being here again, being so down, but never give up and you can continue. Thank you, guys in the box over there, Daddy, Mom, Sasha, Esther . . ."

I put my hand on Venus's back next to me, and I felt her laugh and smile when the presenter congratulated Serena on how she had as many Wimbledon trophies as Venus did. Serena smiled broadly. "I've always wanted everything that Venus had."

The scene below wavered for a moment through my tears. I couldn't see through the lens of my camera. I heard the voices of my daughters all around me, and our family and friends, and the crowd around them, and I felt the fullness of my life. In a special way, I felt real gratitude for all I had. I do not know what prompted it—the girls' tennis victories had always brought out such complex emotions in me that I often hated to watch them play—but that day I found a peace and happiness I had known only a few times before in my life.

What greater value could there be than in finding peace if you've never had it? We search for so many things. When you have peace, you have a serenity about yourself. You're happy with what you do, what you say, the way you look, the way you conduct yourself. You don't have to have the best or the most expensive things. Whatever you have is exactly what you want.

I shook my head and wiped my eyes. It was amazing. All the things I went through and I was still alive. My life could've ended at any time. There were a lot of close calls. Still, for all the wounds, I could walk on my own. For all the insults, I could breathe on my own. I could sit on my tractor on my land and cut my grass as I wished, and no man could tell me different. This was peace, and on this day I could have lain down and died and been happy.

Sitting there, I saw things as I had never seen them before. Seventy years. It was a big life. I felt my heart beat stronger and my chest expand and I wanted to thank all the white people for making me such a strong person. If it wasn't for the life they made me live, I wouldn't have become so tough. I wanted to thank the black people, too, for what they had taught me and how they had helped and even for those who had hurt me. I wanted to thank every person, black and white, for all that they had added to my life. I was the product of each and every experience.

I am seventy years old now and I have a new wife and a new son. Most everyone I know has asked me if I am going to make him a tennis player like Venus and Serena. They want to know if I plan to raise the greatest male tennis player who ever lived. They ask me if I can do it again.

I tell them that is a foolish goal. What do I need with another tennis player? But I am old and crafty and just settling in to write my new plan—complete with directions if I don't get to finish it.

He's going to be a billionaire.

I still dream big.

The Williams Life Triangle

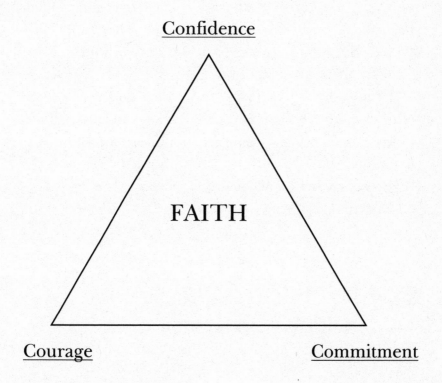

Confidence

FAITH

Courage   Commitment

Top Ten Rules for Success

1. Failing to plan is planning to fail.

2. Always be positive.

3. Confidence is essential to success.

4. Faith is essential to confidence.

5. When you fail, you fail alone.

6. You learn by looking, seeing, and listening.

7. Create theories and test them out.

8. Always have a Plan B.

9. An appreciative child is a blessing.

10. Let no one define you but you.

ACKNOWLEDGMENTS

People have been asking me for many years when I was finally going to write my book. It took the right combination of time and people to accomplish the task. Telling my story would not have been possible without:

Bart Davis, my great writer, who fashioned a narrative out of my story and helped me find my true voice of strength and passion. He justified every trust I placed in him, and I am proud to be his friend and partner.

Chavoita LeSane, my son, who brought us all together and tirelessly kept this project alive when others would have faltered. He deserves great credit.

Robert Gottlieb, my agent, who brought to the project the

enormous resources of Trident Media Group, and his personal wisdom, which never fails.

Malaika Adero, my great senior editor and vice president at Atria Books, whose optimism, skill, and excitement, from the very beginning, powered us through to the end.

Venus and Serena Williams, my daughters, who inspire me and are the reason for it all. My pride in them is constant. My love for them is endless.

Julia Metcalf Williams, my mother, my hero.

Lakeisha Williams, my wife, who encouraged me from the beginning.

Todd Hunter, associate editor at Atria, who kept us all organized.

Mark Gottlieb, of Trident Media Group, who helped at every turn.

Arnon Milchan, my friend who taught me so much.

Alese and Morton Pechter, for their fine photographs.

Larry Bailey, Reginald Sessions, Jan Morrison, Nancy Lyon, Carlos Fleming, Jill Smoller, Robert D. Funderburg, Commissioner Wilson, Adlah Donastorg, Christina Brodwell, Desiree Barber, Alexandra Davis, Jordan Davis, Sharon Davis, Julie Friend, Linda Balcourt, and Sophia Gottlieb.

. . . and the pioneers like Oprah Winfrey, Whoopi Goldberg, Ellen DeGeneres, and Barack and Michelle Obama, among a multitude too vast to name.